# THE GOLDEN TREASURY OF

# EARLY AMERICAN HOUSES

# THE GOLDEN TREASURY OF

# EARLY AMERICAN HOUSES

Richard Pratt

Hawthorn Books, Inc.
Publishers
New York

unston Hall: Through the Drawing Room Door to the Dining Room

ller

THE GOLDEN TREASURY OF EARLY AMERICAN HOUSES

Copyright © 1967 by Hawthorn Books, Inc., 70 Fifth Avenue, New York City 10011. Copyright under International and Pan-American Copyright Conventions. All rights reserved including the right to reproduce this book, or portions thereof, in any form, except for the inclusion of brief quotations in a review. This book was manufactured in the United States of America and published simultaneously in Canada by Prentice-Hall of Canada, Ltd., 1870 Bichmount Road, Scarborough, Ontario. Library of Congress Catalogue Card Number: 67-20791.

DESIGN BY INMAN COOK

First Edition: 1967
Second Printing: 1968

# FOREWORD

One morning in May 1945, I got word that the Goulds wanted to see me upstairs. These were the legendary Goulds of the *Ladies' Home Journal*, my editors. On the way up I wondered, as I always wondered, "What now?"

The day before had been a big one for me. The Museum of Modern Art had given me a party at the opening of a show that filled their whole first floor. The exhibition consisted of a dozen or more large and magically lifelike scale models of experimental houses whose designs I had commissioned, as architectural editor of the *Journal*, from Frank Lloyd Wright, Philip Johnson, Eero Saarinen and others—all the very best. It was my fond belief that when the war was over, "Tomorrow's Small Houses," as the exhibition was called, would be revolutionary in quality and cost, and available to all.

The show had created quite a stir, and was to continue through September, and I thought it would be about this show that the Goulds wanted to see me. But it wasn't. What they had to say was, in effect, "All right, you've had your fling. But we feel you've been having your own way here long enough now. So this is what *we* want you to do . . . We want you to do a series of Early American houses."

*Early American houses!* I couldn't believe my ears. "You mean *old* houses?" I thought

the Goulds must have lost their minds. "But what about our Tomorrow's Small Houses? Are we going to let our readers down?" I moaned. "Just as the *Journal* is about to turn the whole concept of living in this country inside out?" I felt faint. "Do you mind if I sit down a minute?" I asked. "I'm afraid you haven't time," said Mrs. Gould firmly, but with compassion. "You have a lot of things to see, and a lot of pictures to bring back, and I think you had better start traveling."

I staggered across to the Museum. I went all through those marvelous, exciting models, touching each one of them tenderly. I didn't care what the sign said. With tears in my eyes, I ran into Betty Mock and Monroe Wheeler, who had put on the exhibition. "What *is* the matter with you?" they asked. I just couldn't bring myself to tell them. I staggered out and took a taxi to the New York Historical Society. I thought that would be as good a place to start as any. And it was.

From my research in the Historical Society library, I decided that my next stop would be Gunston Hall, with which this book begins. And by the time I had been there along the Potomac, down the James, up the Hudson and across the Connecticut; to Charleston, Portsmouth, Ipswich, and Salem, I had long since come to the conclusion that, as usual, the Goulds were right. They *played* it right, too. They let me do it just the way I wanted.

It was a monumental undertaking. In a few short years enough color plates were collected to fill a book: *A Treasury of Early American Homes*. In no time at all, the first *Treasury* went through many printings. In another four years there were enough color plates for *A Second Treasury of Early American Homes*. Both volumes went into several editions and are still going strong today.

Now *The Golden Treasury of Early American Houses* represents the best of both books, and a lot more. Inman Cook has provided a fresh new typographical setting and an imaginative layout for the occasion, and the publisher a price in keeping with a book twice as big.

These books are not only the most complete picture representations extant of Early American houses, but the only ones of any kind entirely in color. *The Golden Treasury* will have its uses, just as its predecessors have had, for students, decorators, old-house owners, and even, on the sly, for architectural historians. But its greatest audience will be the lovers of Early American houses; it is primarily their pleasure and entertainment that the author had in mind.

I feel that the text is essential to the full enjoyment of the book, and have therefore tried to keep it to the point and make it as brief and easy to read as the pictures are easy to look at.

Since so many owners, custodians and curators are concerned because certain changes have occurred in the furnishings of their houses since some of these pictures were taken, the fact of these changes will be noted either in the captions or in the back of the book.

I acknowledge first of all the previous collaboration of Dorothy Pratt, who died in 1962. From the start, she rang doorbells, fixed flowers, and by smuggling in surreptitious props, gave living presence to many a room afflicted with stultifying period perfectionism. As she often asserted, she did all the work. She did all the dirty work; that part is true; and she got the least out of it.

The photographers worked the hardest, for they had to contend with me. I didn't want them to hang black cloth at the windows, to cut down the sunlight, which they did anyway. Sensitive, delightful Andre Kertesz; that tireless technician Harold Fowler, who never went wrong; Henry Flannery, trained by Steichen; Wesley Balz, the fastidious pro; and finally, the one and only Ezra Stoller, who came to scoff and remained to pray.

A list of those who allowed us to invade and seemingly, at times, to violate their premises, would be as long as the list of houses in this book; and to these forbearing people I am especially indebted, as well might be every reader who gets pleasure from their homes.

And finally, to the Curtis Publishing Company, without whose indispensable and freely donated color plates there would never have been a *Treasury* of any kind – *First, Second,* or *Golden* – to them, the deepest indebtedness of all.

Richard Pratt

1967

Stonington, Connecticut

# INTRODUCTION

A child stood looking down at the Norwich terrier that lives where I live, and, after much thought, finally summed the dog up, "He's like a big dog, only little." That occurred to me just now when I read over the Introduction to the original *Treasury* of 1949. The words still stood, but in too many words. So this is like a long introduction, only short.

The story has nothing to illustrate its beginning. Not a single house survives today that we can be sure was built before 1650. The years running back to the settlement days of Jamestown and Plymouth remain unaccounted for by any examples still standing. A few foundations, some written records, plenty of sound surmises—but that's all we have.

We know this much: Those first few years after 1607 in Virginia, and after 1620 in Massachusetts, were ones in which the so-called Cavaliers in Virginia and the Pilgrim Fathers kept house in the rudest kind of huts and caves. Architecture as such was simply not a thing to which they could turn their attention at the time; emergency building was as much as they could manage. But as soon as they could get around to it, they began to build for greater comfort and protection, and, understandably, for more convenience. With the tools, time to use them, and with essential furnishings and fittings from England, these pioneers began putting up houses that must have begun to look like the earliest houses pictured in the following pages.

The houses in this book were built during the 200 years between 1650 and 1850. All of the houses from Columbia Falls in Maine south to Charleston and Savannah, were built within the region of the English-controlled colonies along the Atlantic seaboard, though many of the houses in the book went up, of course, after that control was taken away. Certain of these later houses indicate the effort that was made during the early days of our independence to shake off our architectural ties with England. How successfully or, more to the point, how unsuccessfully this was accomplished, we shall see. As far as American Provincial is concerned—that is, the houses across the Alleghenies from Kentucky and Tennessee to Natchez and New Orleans, and out to Monterey—it will be apparent that other architectural influences than those stemming directly from England—notably Spanish and French influence from Mexico and the West Indies—were at work in these then remote places.

Thus Early Colonial may now be looked upon in the light of historical building methods and fashions channeled through what was then held by Americans to be the mother country. And by glancing back at the panorama of our past, which these houses so handsomely adorn, we can see how, in their new environment, all these homes of English breeding eventually took on a character that became as American as the people who put them up and occupied them. The New Englanders remembered the humble Elizabethan cottages of the southeastern counties they had left behind; the new Virginians the larger and lesser houses nearer London. And those were the houses they chose to emulate here. When they built from memory, their memory was good; when they built from books, they made their adaptations with delightful mastery.

The Georgian style came ashore first at Williamsburg and spread up the James, from Carter's Grove and the Wythe house to Westover and Berkeley. It laid its loveliness on Charleston, Alexandria, New Castle, and Philadelphia. It covered the colonies with glory, especially where wealth and culture could give it their blessing. Though the responsibility was remotely Christopher Wren's, that architect never came to this country, nor did he ever draw up plans for any houses here.

Instead, the "architects" came here in bundles. They were books from London, inspired by the riches of the English Renaissance and filled with carefully drawn details that colonial craftsmen were quick to carry out. The authors of these handbooks for builders were men to remember and admire – William Halfpenny, Batty Langley, Robert Morris, William Pain, Abraham Swan. More doorways, more mantels, windows, cornices, pediments, and paneling came straight from the pages of these books than from any other source.

Many English craftsmen came as well, like Richard Baylis for Carter's Grove, and William Buckland for Gunston Hall and Mathias Hammond's house in Annapolis. And of course these men spread the good work while they were here, helping the hands of colonial carpenters and adapting the new architecture to colonial towns and countrysides and to the requirements of colonial owners as well. Their help went so far that, with the handbooks for assistance, almost any able builder could draw up and erect a Georgian house. Men of means and taste became architectural amateurs, and gave their Georgian homes a really American personality, as many of the following pictures will show.

Just as there can be no accounting for taste, there was no accounting, at that point in history, for the temper of the times; after the Declaration of Independence was signed, the Revolution won, and the nation on its own, a change in both temper and taste was taking place. And it wasn't long before the change began to show in our houses, first in the homes of intellectuals, and first and most of all in the home of Thomas Jefferson at Monticello.

Thomas Jefferson was the most architecturally conscious statesman this country has ever had – skillful and scholarly, and sternly devoted to the Classical style. That academic devotion had not only an esthetic basis, but an emotional one as well; and on both scores he was scathing in his denunciation of Georgian design. The architecture of Williamsburg filled him with scorn; its prettiness seemed to him a parody of the only architecture worth-while: the noble monuments of Greece and Rome, and the villas of Andrea Palladio. Emotionally he felt that Greece and Rome, apart from the beauty of their buildings, had much in common with our new United States; for Greece and Rome, too, had been young republics. And as a leader of this young republic, a man of extraordinary parts and power, he was able to influence taste with great dispatch and wide effect. His own architecture is among the finest in the American past; but even more than the examples of his work, such as Monticello and the University of Virginia, his compelling passion for the Classical mode was the force that helped to change the tide of American taste.

Other forces were moving concurrently, and the most important of these were of English origin. There was Lord Byron, who with a poet's pervasiveness was making the world aware of the plight of Greece, then under attack by the barbarous Turks. There were the measured drawings that James Stuart and Nicholas Revett had been making of Classical remains in Greece and Italy. These drawings – great folios of engravings – appeared in London, adding fuel to Byron's flames. That was all we needed, not only to complete our identification with those ancient young republics, but to provide us with the means of reproducing here what seemed in the circumstances a most appropriate style of architecture. The means of reproducing that

architecture were facilitated once again by the appearance in London, and soon thereafter in America, notably by Asher Benjamin in Boston, of builder's handbooks; but this time putting pure Classicism to work – at least as pure as possible, considering the transitions that had to be made from ancient temples to contemporary houses, and from monumental masonry to domestic wood and plaster.

In the hands of Jefferson and a gathering group of able architects, this Classical urge produced a style of undeniable dignity, and in the later work of McIntire in Salem and other architect-craftsmen elsewhere, it achieved an eloquent beauty. In fact, it became for a while what many consider the most authentically American manner of building, from mansions like Andalusia to temple-like cottages. But as its popularity spread and the manner began to lose whatever meaning it had, the Greek Revival, with some notable exceptions, grew quainter and quainter, weaker and weaker. A Gothic Revival, to become equally quaint, was coming to life in England; Ruskin was writing, and disciples here were stirring with new ideas. It was nearing 1850, and the Romantic Era was arriving, with an assortment of theatrical styles to decorate the Industrial Age.

What followed was fascinating. But my curtain has come down. And already this is getting to look like a short introduction, only long.

# TABLE OF CONTENTS

# Gunston Hall

With the rush of stylish housebuilding that opened the 1750's, Virginia plantation owners started a run on English joiners and woodcarvers. The owners already had plenty of competent colonial carpenters and masons (most of them Negroes) and plenty of plans and precedents for well-proportioned finely fenestrated mansions. (The basic floor plan was set; two rooms on either side of a central hallway.) They had all the wood they wanted for lumber, and all the clay they needed for brick. What was in short supply were talented English-trained craftsmen who could finish off the houses with fine displays of paneling and carving, inside and out, but mainly within. Carter Burwell had the English master carver Richard Baylis do Carter's Grove, and various other owners secured various other master craftsmen from England for *their* houses. (Besides Carter's Grove, men must have been brought over for the Moore, for Kenmore, Wilton, the Wythe, and for Gunston Hall.) It remained for George Mason to bring over William Buckland. And what Buckland did for Gunston Hall is one of, if not *the*, finest examples of craftsmanship and designing of colonial times.

The Bedroom

*Stoller*

When George Mason was getting ready to build his house, he was thirty years old, had been married five years, was trustee of Alexandria, justice of Fairfax County court and vestryman of Truro Parish. He had taken possession of his great Dogue's Neck plantation nine years before, on coming of age, and now, at the same time, to the month almost, that George Washington became tenant and master of Mount Vernon, a few miles up the Potomac, Mason started to build. He was wealthy and wise, but healthy he was not. Already he was troubled by gout, and he was to be plagued by it, more and more, the rest of his life.

It is quite a coincidence that just as Henry Hollyday, in Talbot County, Maryland (see page 62), was writing to his brother in London, "I have made this summer 80 or 90 thousand bricks in order to build next summer. . . . Please send me a Joyner in the spring," Mason, with his bricks made, and with his oak and pine all cut and stacked was writing *his* brother in London to find a well-trained joiner to help finish the house on the Dogue's Neck plantation.

William Buckland was born in Oxford on August 14, 1734. What a time for a joiner to be born! For a talented young man, the opportunities for training had never been better in England than they were in the early part of the eighteenth century, when the architecture in fashion could make use of the finest artistry in woodcarving and joinery. And by a stroke of luck, the opportunity was waiting for William when he was fourteen; his uncle, James Buckland, being a master in those arts, was practicing in London. The uncle had the nephew as an apprentice for seven years, and then the young man was on his own, just as Thomson Mason appeared with George Mason's appeal in his pocket. The papers were drawn, and Mason and Buckland set out for Virginia.

The agreement is printed here to show the conditions of indenture during that era.

The Library

*Stoller*

## Indenture of Service, Buckland to Mason

*This Indenture, Made the Fourth Day of August in the Twenty ninth Year of the Reign of our Sovereign Lord George Second King of Great Britain, Etc., And in the Year of our Lord One Thousand Seven Hundred and fifty five—between William Buckland of Oxford Carpenter & Joiner of the one Part and Thomson Mason of London Esqr.—of the other Part, Witnesseth . . . That He the said William Buckland shall and will, as a faithful Covenant Servant, well and truly serve the said Thomson Mason, his Executors or Assigns in the Plantation of Virginia beyond the Seas, for the Space of Four Years, next ensuing his Arrival in the said Plantation in the Employment of a Carpenter & Joiner. And the said Willm Buckland doth hereby Covenant and Declare himself, now to be the Age of Twenty two years and Single and no Covenant or Contracted Servant to any other Person or Persons, And the said Thomson Mason for himself his Executors or Assigns, in Consideration thereof, doth hereby Covenant, Promise and Agree to and with the said Willm Buckland his Executors, and Assigns, that He the said Thomson Mason his . . . Executors or Assigns, shall and will at his or their own proper Costs and Charges, with what convenient Speed they may, carry and convey or cause to be carried and conveyed over unto the said Plantation, the said Wm Buckland and from Henceforth, and during the said Voyage, and also during the said Term shall and will at the like Costs and Charges, provide for and allow the said Wm Buckland all necessary Meat, Drink, Washing, Lodging, fit and convenient for him as Covenant Servants in such Cases are usually provided for and allowed and pay and allow the said William Buckland Wages or Salary at the Rate of Twenty Pounds Sterling per Annum Payable Quarterly.*

The Chinese Chippendale Dining Room

21

Four years later, at the end of his indenture, George Mason inscribed the following on the back of the document:

*The within named William Buckland came into Virginia with my Brother Thomson Mason who engaged him in London and had a very good Character of him there; during the time he lived with me he had the entire Direction of the Carpenters & Joiners Work of a large House; & having behaved very faithfully in my Service, I can with great justice recommend him to any Gentleman that may have occasion to employ him, as an honest sober diligent Man, & I think a complete Master of the Carpenter's & Joiner's Business both in Theory & Practice.*

                     *G. Mason*
                   *8th Novr., 1759*

(Notation in Buckland's hand:)
        *W Buckland was born*
        *Augt ye 14th 1734*        *1773*
                                   *1734*
                                     *39*

After Buckland had completed his work at Gunston, he eventually settled in Annapolis, where he created, among other fine houses, his Maryland masterpiece, the Hammond-Harwood house shown on pages 78 and 79. His portrait by Charles Willson Peale was begun in 1774, the year Buckland died at forty, presumably at Annapolis. (Peale did not complete the portrait until 1787, by which time Buckland was hardly remembered.)

An enormous cupola extensively changed the outer appearance of Gunston Hall when it was installed after the Civil War. The cupola was removed in 1913. Today, Gunston's complete restoration has renewed the fame of its architect. We know very little of him, apart from what we can assume from his portrait and from the inventory of his estate, totaling about eight hundred pounds. He did once appear before a grand jury on charges of profanity, which was considered one of the more serious crimes. Buckland, although he had been an indentured servant himself, acquired indentured servants of his own. He left no descendants of his name. He left his library of architectural books, but what happened to it nobody knows. Fortunately, he left something more priceless, and after many years of obscurity for Gunston Hall, Buckland's fame is once again assured.

The Palladian Drawing Room

*Stoller*

# Kenmore at Fredericksburg

Colonel Fielding Lewis built Kenmore in 1752, for his bride Betty, George Washington's only sister. In the operation of the Revolutionary arsenal in Fredericksburg, Lewis exhausted his personal fortune, with the result that after his death the property was held for taxes. Washington then stepped in to save the house for his sister. It then managed quite well under various owners until the 1920's, when two Fredericksburg women with extraordinary spirit and enterprise organized a group of local ladies who not only saved the house, but gathered sufficient funds from far and near to effect its beautiful restoration.

The Boxwood Allée

*Balz*

The plaster work of the ceiling and overmantel in the drawing room, executed by talented Hessian prisoners of war, is the finest of the whole colonial period.

This was Betty's bedroom, and here, on her four-poster, she found her brother in his muddy boots, resting after his ride back from the Yorktown surrender.

The dining room mantelpiece carving is the Washington crest, "The Swan and the Crown," the triple urn a Lewis possession. The portrait is of Colonel Lewis.

The music room was made the largest and most elegant in the mansion for a family that went in whole-heartedly for musical evenings.

# Woodlawn

Lawrence Lewis, Washington's nephew, born at Kenmore, and his wife Nelly, Martha Washington's granddaughter, started building this beautiful house in 1802, from plans by the Capitol architect William Thornton, on lands of the Mount Vernon estate inherited from the General. Its Federal stylishness starts with the entrance front and continues through room after room. The woodwork of the dining room is grained to simulate mahogany. Grained, too, with great effect, are the doors in Lorenzo's bedroom on the left below and the girl's room on the right.

*Stoller*

# WASHINGTON

The city of Washington was created by the first Congress from sections of land contributed by Maryland and Virginia and contained both Alexandria, Virginia, and Georgetown, Maryland. Alexandria managed in 1846 to return to Virginia. Georgetown, therefore, now provides most of the city's best early houses, of which Dumbarton, started in 1799, is the most resplendent.

Called by the late Fiske Kimball "one of the very finest and most beautiful houses in the United States," Dumbarton was begun in 1799 by Samuel Jackson, finished in 1803 by Joseph Nourse and named Bellevue by Charles Carroll, who bought it in 1813. In August, a year later, when the British attacked the capital, Carroll drove down from Bellevue to the White House to beg Dolley Madison to hurry; the British were only minutes away. She barely made it, lugging a large portrait of Washington. It was the National Society of the Colonial Dames of America who named the house Dumbarton in 1928, after they had restored it and made it their National Headquarters.

The Lindens is an earlier house, but a rather recent arrival in Washington, having been brought down from Danvers, Massachusetts, in the 1930's. It was named from the grove of trees which grew around it in Danvers.

*Photograph from Houses, History & People, by Richard Pratt, courtesy M. Evans & Co.*

## Dumbarton

Dumbarton has been furnished to reflect the fashion of the late eighteenth and early nineteenth centuries. The painting in the music room above the fireplace is Washington's niece Harriet with a boy who is probably Harriet's brother Lawrence. On the left is the dining-room fireplace. In the library chamber on the right above, the field bed is New England Hepplewhite, as is the mahogany and maple bureau in the corner. The bandbox is early-nineteenth-century New York, the rug an Aubusson.

32

## The Lindens from Danvers

Piece by piece the house came down from the Bay State, where it was built in 1754. The house is a masterpiece of colonial carpentry craftsmanship, with its balustraded gambrel roof, its pedimented and pilastered façade, and particularly its front siding which was grooved and sanded to resemble ashlar-cut masonry, as was done at Mount Vernon. The outstanding architectural feature inside is the famous stair hall, decorated with hand-blocked French wallpapers. The carving of the newel post and the spiral carving of the balusters are further triumphs of colonial artistry.

The owner has made her house a masterpiece of restoration in the best sense of period perfectionism. Everything is mid-eighteenth century. "Not even the design for a curtain valance," she contends, "is later than 1754." The drawing room exemplifies this. Its original woodwork covers the walls from floor to ceiling. The furniture—Queen Anne and Chippendale—would have been the last word when the house was built; the prize, perhaps, is the finely formed American sofa. A telephone that tinkles faintly from the closet in the corner is the only anachronism.

# DOWN THE JAMES

The James is the great Georgian river of the Colonies; Westover, whose closest neighbors are Shirley and Berkeley, is its prize. Wilton, Ampthill and Tuckahoe are in and out of Richmond up the river. Brandon is lower down on the other side, and Carter's Grove is below Williamsburg. That celebrated Georgian capital of the Colony is not on the river. It was settled well back from the James, over toward the York, where it is more than ever the popular focal point of the region.

Jefferson and the Randolphs used the river road in their comings and goings between Williamsburg and Richmond. Before them, the first William Byrd had traveled by the river more often than on the land. He owned both sides of it; in fact, he had owned all the land on which Richmond now stands. With his wealth, taste, and intelligence, he was the ideal tidewater aristocrat. His son William inherited all those attributes and enlarged upon them. He wrote with style and wit becoming one of the foremost colonial authors. In 1729, in a letter to a friend in London, he said, "I intend to set about building a very good house." This was something of an understatement for what, in fact, was the masterpiece on the opposite page.

*Pratt*

The morning sun across the James lights up one of the loveliest façades in America and shines on one of the most beautiful doorways in the world.

*Balz*

# Millwood

Millwood, a dozen miles west of Richmond, in Powhatan County, has the aristocratic touch: crisp, clean lines, sharply defined dormers, big, buttressed outside chimneys—all betokening the Old Dominion. In a state where Georgian splendor was the eighteenth-century rule, Millwood took simplicity for its text and became a gentle house in every sense of the word. The living room typifies a Virginia country interior of that era.

*Pratt*

# Wilton Transported

Here again we can admire not only the virtuosity of colonial craftsmanship, but the wizardry of the modern builder. For when Wilton's original situation down the river became hopeless in the thirties, the house was taken apart, brought fourteen miles up to this commanding site above the James, and then put together again, to be better than when it was built in 1753, and more beautifully furnished—as the nursery here, and the articles on the following pages, will show.

*Pratt*

*Stoller*

39

In this glorious parlor, as in every other room in the house, including alcoves and closets, the walls are paneled in heart pine from floor to ceiling. Over the fireplace is a portrait of William Randolph III, builder of Wilton, and over the Chippendale sofa, a portrait of his daughter Elizabeth. After the ownership of William III came those of Peyton, another William, Robert, and Kate.

In the library a Queen Anne mirror hangs above the oxbow chest. The Peale portrait of Washington now hangs in the Washington room, where the General used to sleep.

*Balz*

*Balz*

# Brandon, on the Southern Bank

Built in 1756, Brandon is one of the most handsomely composed of all the houses along the James. Still lived in and actively maintained, the estate remains a working plantation. The Thomas Sully portrait over the drawing-room fireplace is of Peyton Randolph of Williamsburg, statesman cousin of the Peyton at Wilton. The paneling and carving are the wonders of a room that is filled with such fine things as the Sheraton sofa and the magnificent Aubusson. There is talk that Jefferson may have had something to do with the porch. He was certainly a frequent visitor, as were Washington and Henry Clay. Williamsburg wasn't far away.

The pineapple finial on the peak of the roof is perfect. whoever did it.

# IN AND OUT OF WILLIAMSBURG

The Williamsburg of George Wythe, Washington, Jefferson, Henry Clay, and the Randolphs will never be seen again as it was from 1699 to 1779, when it was the capital of Virginia. The streets are no longer ankle-deep in mud or dust; cows, pigs, and chickens no longer roam at random through the town; and the only celebrities to be seen are visiting V.I.P.'s. The Palace is new, the Capitol is new, and so is the Raleigh Tavern, where the Revolutionary patriots gathered in their muddy boots. Almost everything in the restored area that was not eighteenth-century has been taken away; there remains at least one Federal house, too fine to sacrifice to period perfectionism. Otherwise, all that remain are the restorations, to which have been added truly meticulous reconstructions. It is the most popular attraction of its kind in the country, as well as the most highly publicized and the most richly endowed.

When Jamestown was burned during Bacon's Rebellion in 1676, Williamsburg, still known as Middle Plantation, became the temporary seat of government for Virginia. Poor Jamestown! Ever since it was settled in 1607, it had suffered more than its share of misfortune. Even so, it again became the seat of Government until finally it was burned for good in 1698. Its citizens might have rebuilt still another time but instead they moved on to Williamsburg. They just couldn't stand the "musketees" any longer.

## The Wythe House

The Wythe House was built in 1755, by
Richard Taliaferro as a wedding present,
it has been said, for his daughter and her
husband George Wythe, who taught law at
the nearby College of William and Mary,
where Jefferson had been a student. Once
when the Wythes were away in Philadelphia, the Jeffersons stayed there. They
found a note from Wythe: "The conven-
iency of my house and servants and furniture to you and Mrs. Jefferson adds not
a little to their value in my estimation."

*Pratt*

# The Nicolson House

This house is a few steps on York Street from the restoration area, and has been acquired by Colonial Williamsburg, but is still (as of 1967) privately occupied, as are many houses in the reservation area. In 1766, it was the home of Robert Nicolson, a prominent townsman and tailor of Williamsburg. In that year, he advertised "genteel lodgings" with breakfast and good stabling for "gentlemen who attend the General Courts and Assembly."

The Nicolson house stands on York Street and is the easternmost building in the Historic Area which encompasses the colonial town of Williamsburg.

Although now owned by Colonial Williamsburg, this house was owned for many years by James L. Cogar, who is now director of Shakertown at Pleasant Hill, Kentucky. The furniture shown here is now, according to Mr. Cogar, "in another old house, which, by tradition, is the oldest stone house west of the Alleghenies."

# The Brush-Everard House

The reproduction of blue colonial wallpaper sets the tone for the stunning color treatment in the rest of the downstairs bedroom restoration

48

Two of the most entertaining houses in town stand on opposite sides of the Palace Green; the Wythe on the west, the Brush-Everard on the east. What makes them so entertaining? For one thing, the people. George Wythe was a colonial figure of the first rank, as was his whole townhouse establishment; its grounds and dependencies are as fascinating as the mansion itself. Across the Green, the various eighteenth-century occupants of the small frame house were men of local importance. John Brush, a gunsmith and armorer, was the first keeper of the powder magazine. When Brush built the original house, two rooms to a floor, Henry Cary, who owned it for a while, was completing the Palace. Cary sold it in 1742 to William Dering, a dancing master and artist. Then, just about at the time that the Wythe house was going up, Thomas Everard bought what by then could have been called the old Brush house. He was County Clerk and clerk of the General Court, and became a mayor of Williamsburg. "Much of the enlargement of the property," according to Colonial Williamsburg, "dates from the period of his ownership." The house acquired two wings in back, giving it a U-shaped plan. Its fine paneling and wallpaper were unusual and expensive in Williamsburg houses. It could well be assumed that Everard was responsible for these improvements. The Williamsburg people have chosen to restore and furnish it in the pre-Revolutionary period of Everard's occupancy, including reproductions of the colonial wallpaper and a restoration of the gardens and the grounds, with all their dependencies, down to the two sequestered privies on either side of the great boxwood allee. The Wythe House and grounds are more extensive, inside and out, but the Brush-Everard is just as entertaining in its own way.

In Everard's parlor the hangings and upholstery are of red watered moreen, a wool material that has held its original brilliance now for two centuries.

# Carter's Grove Plantation

This magnificent colonial mansion faces out over the James from the topmost of its terraced lawns, six miles below Williamsburg. It is justly famous for its paneled drawing rooms and extraordinary stair hall. The main central section was built between 1750 and 1755. The construction was undertaken by the Williamsburg team of John Minetree, mason, and John Wheatley, carpenter. At the same time, the latter was making repairs to the Governor's Palace and working on the new Capitol building in Williamsburg. The English master carver Richard Baylis was brought over to Virginia to complete the fine interior work. All the timbers and framing were cut from forests on the property, as was all the famous pine, walnut, and poplar paneling. Even the bricks were fired on the site, from clay that was dug from the fields.

Carter's Grove has been acquired from the estate of the late Mrs. Archibald M. McCrea by Sealantic Fund, a Rockefeller-supported philanthropic organization, and is maintained and exhibited by Colonial Williamsburg.

Carter Burwell was proprietor of the plantation during the time the principal construction was done. His taste produced the general idea, and Baylis was responsible for the design and execution of the magnificent interiors.

In this other paneled drawing room, it has been said that a duel was fought: one killed, one wounded. The pictures of the drawing rooms and the hallway were taken during the ownership of Mrs. McCrea.

The carved staircase and the main hallway, completely paneled in pine, create a stirring approach to Carter's Grove's great pair of drawing rooms.

52

*Stoller*

# Hill's Farm near Accomac

Hill's Farm is one of the more splendid Shore houses, seen here with sheep grazing on its lawns, and its encroaching tidewater creek. Its morning room (left), and its dining room glimpsed beyond, hint at its extremely stylish interiors. It is very early indeed—built in 1697, they say, by a man named Richard Drummond, on the farm of his grandfather Hill.

Virginia's Eastern Shore is the oldest community in the state, except for Jamestown itself, whose people often explored the peninsula, making settlements that became permanent. Eyre Hall and Wharton, like Hill's Farm, are large, important houses, but among the smaller houses, often of great age, a tradition of building has developed that the house expands in a straight line as additions are made, ending up in a style known locally as "Big House, Little House, Colonnade, and Kitchen."

# Wharton near Modest Town

Wharton holds the double honor of having been both an extraordinary deviation from local design traditions, and a smuggler's residence deluxe. An eighteenth-century expatriate from Philadelphia, John Wharton, by his subversive skills and great successes, was able to build for himself a noble Philadelphia mansion in one of the best locations on the ocean side of the Shore. It survived many decades of squatter tenancy without a blemish to become the monumental pride of the peninsula. It's as fascinating a house as will be found anywhere, superbly maintained with appropriate esteem by its devoted owners.

The dining room, with its Adam mantel in black enamel, opens into the drawing room at the right, and into the hall with its extraordinary three-story staircase.

# THE EASTERN SHORE OF MARYLAND

For Marylanders, county names have deeper significance than anywhere else in the country. In this sense the area is rather like England. In the case of the tidewater counties, the feeling that certain names evoke communicates itself even to outsiders who love the early houses, towns, and tidewater scenes. We will look at three counties: Queen Annes, Cecil, and Talbot. Talbot (pronounced Tallbut) seems for some, in fact, a treasury of Early American houses all by itself.

The yellow sofas in Blakeford's big drawing room are Baltimore Sheraton, the portrait between them is a Sully, and the grospoint rug is from Portugal.

*Pratt*

# Blakeford

This is in Queen Annes County, on the Chester River, in a tidewater setting enhanced by gardens and grand old trees. Built in 1833, for owners who liked to entertain their friends from Annapolis and Baltimore across the Bay, it still makes a point of fulfilling that function. Many of the beautiful old tidewater houses, like Blakeford, are hidden away up the countless creeks and rivers that cut into the eastern shore of Chesapeake Bay. They were meant to be approached by water, and even today the landward way is often harder to travel.

The Hepplewhite hunt board, against the far wall of the dining room, is one of Blakeford's rarest pieces. Over the mantel is a portrait of the owner's great-uncle, by Gilbert Stuart.

# Ratcliffe Manor

In 1755, Henry Hollyday, of Readbourne Rectified nearby, in Talbot County, wrote his brother in London, "I have made this summer 80 or 90 thousand bricks in order to build next summer . . . Please send me a Joyner in the Spring." The fireplace wall of Ratcliffe's paneled drawing room shows what a good joiner Henry's brother sent.

*Pratt*

*Balz*

The room is enchanting in its summer attire; the portrait is a Henry Raeburn.

The roof lines show signs of the widening done in the early 1800's.

The restoration of the kitchen disclosed the brick floor, the beams, and even the fireplace.

## Crooked Intention

When Hugh Sherwood obtained the deed for this land on Talbot County's San Domingo Creek in 1681, he named it to mean that his intention to return to England had been changed, or bent, by the beauty of the place where, a few years later, he built this house. The furniture of the paneled living room, except for the Windsor chair, is all eighteenth-century Chippendale and Sheraton.

*Balz*

# Boston Cliff

This is a very early eighteenth-century house. Like
nearby Troth's Fortune, which is very late seventeenth-
century, it is near the Choptank. Both houses, which are
in Talbot County, are known as the North Choptank type,
with high gables, low eaves, delicate dormers, impressive
chimneys, and colorful names. (A book could be written
about Maryland house names.) The Boston Cliff drawing
room, below, is done with brilliance and formality; the
woodwork is painted as it well may have been painted
originally, when bright colors were popular in these small
manor houses. The Queen Anne walnut secretary with
mirrors is a Philadelphia piece. The portraits in both
rooms are of the Virginia ancestors of the owners.

*Stoller*

68

The Hepplewhite bow-front sideboard is eighteenth-century English, as is the mirror above it.

*Stoller*

## Troth's Fortune

*Pratt*

On the other side of this house that William Troth built, is an engaged staircase tower that betrays the great age of the house by its almost medieval nature. The delicate details of the living room paneling seem almost ethereal because of the subtlety of the coloring.

## Kennersly: 1704

Not far from Blakeford, in Queen Annes County, the entrance front of Kennersly faces the land approach. The far side looks out over the Chester River. The Anchorage, below, is on Miles River, in Talbot County, where in 1783 the owner, the pastor of St. Michael's parish, ran a race track behind his chapel.

## The Anchorage

# Myrtle Grove near Easton

Someone said affectionately of Myrtle Grove that it "strikes a true balance between neglect and ostentation"; an oblique way of describing its extraordinary charm and rare atmosphere—the result, in part, of its having remained in the appreciative possession of one family from the time the first frame portion was built in 1724. It stands on the bank of the Miles River, near Easton, in Talbot County, a few minutes' sail upstream from the Anchorage and a long way around by road.

In the hallway of Myrtle Grove, below, with its beautiful doorway and cornice, hangs the portrait by Charles Willson Peale of Judge Robert Goldsborough, his wife, and two children, who were the occupants of the house when the brick section was added to the original part in 1790. The dining room, right, in the older frame section of the house, is filled with heirloom furniture. An earlier Judge Goldsborough is over the fireplace.

*Balz*

# Bohemia in Cecil County

Cecil County is at the northern end of the Eastern Shore, cornering on Pennsylvania to the north and Delaware to the east. The bricks of Bohemia's land front are laid in all-header bond, many of the bricks with dark glazed ends, creating a striking effect. The house faces the Bohemia, both house and river deriving their names from the native land of an early important Bohemian settler, Augustine Herman. Creating an even more striking effect is the Chippendale staircase, with no two balusters alike, and the molded plaster decorations of the whole hallway, above and below.

Again, in the living room of Bohemia, molded plaster is the material that creates the cornices and the Georgian-Baroque mantelpiece from floor to ceiling. The Dresden figurine on the mantel shelf is one of Benjamin Franklin, and the bottle beside the old celestial globe is Stiegel.

# IN AND OUT OF ANNAPOLIS

Annapolis became the capital of Maryland in 1695, and in time, one of the most beautiful towns in America. Still the former, it would still be the latter if it weren't for the wires. The truth is, Annapolis, with its narrow streets, is still an eighteenth-century town, which the twentieth century treats with its customary contempt. A great beauty boom began here in 1750, with the building of the Ridout House, followed by the Brice, and climaxed in 1774, when William Buckland, of Gunston Hall fame, completed the Chase-Lloyd House, above, and built the Hammond-Harwood House across the street. Lloyd wanted his house to be the highest in town, so that he could look out across the Chesapeake to his beloved Eastern Shore.

# The Hammond-Harwood House

Mathias Hammond left the design of everything to William Buckland. He wanted his home to be a modest town house in appearance, but for his bride, he wanted it to be the most beautiful in Annapolis. Buckland did both. He gave it two semi-octagonal wings connected by hyphens to the two-story main building, a superbly balanced composition. He made the celebrated entrance doorway a masterpiece of floral garlands, as though he were doing it for the bride, which indeed he was. He lavished all his skill as a woodcarver on the paneling inside, and particularly in the dining room, just as he had outdone himself in his architectural conception of the whole house. And Colonel Lloyd could still see out over it and across to the Shore.

*Balz*

The dining room is adorned with window and doorway carvings and Chippendale furniture.

# Tulip Hill on South River

Anne Arundel is the county of the fine Annapolis houses—Tulip Hill and a host of others. We will treat Tulip Hill, one of the Maryland greats. It stands in a grove of tulip poplars, on a lovely rise of land overlooking a tidewater expanse. It was built for Samuel Galloway and his wife Anne, who died in childbirth just before the house was finished. (Its symbolic Cupid had already been carved in the pediment of the porch.) Galloway remained a widower. He prospered in the foreign trade with his fleet of ships; among them the *Tulip*, the *Grove*, the *Planter*, the *Swallow*. A Quaker, he established a famous racing stable and entertained tremendously. It was George Washington's habit to drop in for dinner after the races and hobnob with the county nabobs, whose names would still be nice to drop, if there were room in this text. Instead, there is this stunning entrance hall to mention, leading under the double pendant archway to the staircase and the view out over the terraces and down to the river. The wide shell-crowned cupboard with its butterfly shelves is filled with a rare collection of milk-glazed *blanc de chine*.

The drawing room is a reminder of the owners' long residence in China, with its magnificent screen, handpainted on silk, the bronze goose incense burner, and the rare Peking enamels on the mantelshelf against the full-paneled wall.

*Stoller*

*Pratt*

# Holly Hill

One of the best of Maryland's late seventeenth-century manor houses, this is also one of the most handsome. Like many of these earliest tidewater houses, Holly Hill's legend concerns a pirate and a secret passage. Hogarth was his name, and the passage ran to Herring Bay, half a mile away. The entrance can still be seen in the cellar. The fireplace wall of the second floor parlor has been marbleized in an amazing way, with a landscape painting on its chimney piece.

*Balz*

# Cremona in St. Mary's County

The fine Federal mansion called Cremona, built in 1819, stands in its grove of great willow oaks on the shore of the Patuxent in St. Mary's, the county of St. Mary's City, the capital of Maryland before the King decided upon Annapolis. It is the most southern of the southern Maryland counties, with a long shore line on the Potomac, and with a rich architectural tradition extending from the late seventeenth century to the time of Cremona, one of Maryland's last, great, early houses. Just back of where the camera was placed for the picture above, the fields are filled with shiny black cattle, and between the fields and the large house lawn runs one of the longest ha-ha's (a sunken fence invisible from the house) in the country. In the house is one of the most staggering *staircases* in the country, a hanging double stairway, to be seen on the next page, that fills the three-story hall like a towering abstraction. It has often been said that stair builders were the prima donnas of the carpentry craft.

# TO THE TIDEWATER CAROLINAS

Most of the settlements along the coast, from Virginia south, were made by sea; certainly the places represented here: New Bern, Charleston, Seabrook Island, Savannah. Just to touch upon them, it is entertaining to think that the development of New Bern was largely due to Yankee sea-traders from up the Connecticut River, who sailed out of Long Island Sound on a regular route to the West Indies, thence to New Bern, and back to Connecticut, accounting in part for the New England look of this entrancing town.

Charleston, lower down, was given an aristocratic start when Charles II granted great tracts of land to a group of noble lords, his friends, one of whom, Sir Anthony Ashley Cooper, gave the names Ashley and Cooper to the two rivers that join where the city now stands. Then twenty years later the Huguenot refugees from France added *their* names and their aristocratic tone. Seabrook was a plantation with a strong Charleston connection when it was easier to reach by water than by land. And of course Savannah, still further down the coast, a settlement-by-the-sea if ever there was one, became the most important seaport south of Philadelphia, with such strong London ties that the English styling of its old squares and the houses that border them is still the city's most glamorous attraction.

# IN AND OUT OF CHARLESTON

An even more remarkable thing about old Charleston than her pastel streets, graceful churches, elegant houses, and exquisite interiors is the fact that any of these enchantments still remain. No other colonial city has suffered such a profusion of calamities of so many different kinds. Time after time, fire has left great areas of Charleston in ashes, and twice it has been raked by ruinous bombardment—once by the British in the Revolution, and once by the Northern cannons in the Civil War. Not to be outdone, nature has forever hurled fierce hurricanes and tornadoes at the town and has even rocked it with more than its quota of earthquakes. Yet all the large and small streets that lie between South Battery and Broad are still richly lined with relics of the past. This architecture tells the story of a town that already had a cosmopolitan culture two centuries ago—English, French, and West Indian. Yet the final effect is wholly Charleston. Outside Charleston, the famous old plantation houses and fabulous gardens of the Low Country unfold another part of the same performance.

In each elegant old house there are, as a rule, two separate drawing rooms: one upstairs, one down. The one upstairs was generally the more formal, with the finer woodwork and the more choice furnishings. It was the one from which the hostess said good-by to her departing guests, the host greeting and taking leave of them downstairs at the door.

The Christopher Wren-like spire of St. Michael's towers above the sidewalk flower sellers of Meeting Street to punctuate almost every view of old Charleston.

Pratt

87

# The Gibbes House

Facing out across the water from South Battery, the Gibbes House is one of Charleston's great residential monuments. The main floor stands a full story above the street, as though creating an excuse for the magnificent double staircase that decorates its Adamesque Federal façade. The music room on the top floor, shown at the right, is the *chef d'oeuvre* of the mansion. Behind the house is a garden of white azaleas, great live oaks, and low servants' quarters and stables with shiny old tile roofs.

The Chippendale woodwork gives this drawing room—one of a pair—a Chinese flavor.

*Pratt*

An outstanding example in this country of an Adam-style town house, the Russell House of 1807 is now the quarters of the Charleston Historic Foundation.

*Stoller*

The floating staircase leads from the downstairs drawing room to the upstairs one opposite.

# The Nathaniel Russell House

In the Russell house the first-floor drawing room is the formal reception room; its decoration is of almost classic formality. Upstairs, the drawing room is more ornate, yet socially relaxed. The cornices are all encrusted with delicate Adam ornamentation.

# Brandford-Horry: 1751

In the downstairs drawing room of this house, below left, the fireplace is faced with Delft. The muted brilliance of the Chinese rug and the lute-like forms of the Hepplewhite furniture further contribute to the tone and lightness of this stylish reception parlor. Upstairs the carving, the paneling, and the golden patina of the drawing-room walls are one of the triumphs of Charleston interiors. The lighter wood is native cypress, whose beauty has been enhanced by years of hand rubbing. The darker woods are tulip and mahogany. The china in both rooms is some of the finest in Charleston.

93

## The Young-Johnson House

Every nook and cranny of the upstairs drawing room in this charming (small for Charleston) house of 1770 contains something rare and exciting. The Young-Johnson House was obviously the home of a connoisseur collector. The boy in the painting above the mantel is the owner's uncle as a child. Thomas Sully chose to paint him wearing the same dilapidated straw hat in which the painter posed his own son for the famous portrait now in Boston. Sully grew up here, and did much of his best work in Charleston.

*Pratt*

94

# The John Stuart House

The upstairs drawing room in this Georgian house, built by Colonel John Stuart on Tradd Street in 1772, represents most faithfully its original character and quality. Everything here—paneling, overmantel, pedimented doorways, fireplace, and plasterwork—is the remarkable reproduction of the original shell which is now in the Kansas City Art Museum.

*Pratt*

## The Staats House

This is one of the houses that survived the fire of 1740, and stands on one of the very rare grants of land made by the Lords Proprietors to a woman, Elizabeth Willis. Even more noteworthy for its beauty, inside out out, it was fortunately built to last, with brick walls twenty-nine inches thick, covered with oyster-shell stucco. It is paneled throughout with its original heart cypress. It also has a ghost: a young poet who, in 1786, fought a duel outside the doorway over the famous actress Perdita. He was brought inside the house to die. Standing next to the old First Baptist Church (by Robert Mills) the house shows typical Charleston piazzas, the street doorway leading into the lower piazza.

Within the off-white paneled drawing room are rare pieces of Hepplewhite, Chippendale, and Sheraton furniture, an Adam mantel, and an extraordinary old Tabriz animal carpet.

The Staats dining room chairs are American Regency, of mountain ash; the portrait is by Benjamin West.

# A Glance at New Bern

The recently reconstructed Tryon's Palace, next to the charm of the town itself, is New Bern's chief attraction, but the fine Federal houses proclaim the town's great sea-trading period, typified by the Smallwood-Ward House of 1812.

*Pratt*

The Smallwood dining room features a pair of identical tables under identical mirrors in the identical alcoves.

*Balz*

## Mulberry Plantation

Looking out over the Low Country, this remarkable plantation house with four low corner towers, called flankers, of Jacobean Baroque, acquired its opulence from the richness of the ancient rice and indigo fields down the river. Thomas Broughton, an early planter-politician, built it in 1714. The flankers have long been the cause of controversy. Some say they had military significance. (Ancient cannons have been uncovered from what is now the lawn.) Others point out that slender slits in the brick would have offered better protection. Still others don't care, but like them for the way they look.

## Seabrook Plantation

Sea Island cotton, rice, and indigo were the crops that provided the wherewithal for William Seabrook to build this Adamesque Low Country plantation house in 1810, on Edisto Island, fifty miles below Charleston by road, thirty miles by sea. The dramatic feature of the house is the double-staircase hall with its view through to the water.

*Pratt*

102

The restoration of the drawing room, right, typical of the whole house, is also typical of the taste of its owner, who also owns Spite House in Maine. The portrait is of his mother. The dining room, below, is dominated by the triple doorway and its semi-elliptical transom.

*Pratt*

# A GLANCE AT SAVANNAH

The finest of the houses that frame Savannah's fascinating squares range from Regency to the Classical and Gothic Revivals. The squares, their surrounding façades forming a frieze of soft yellows, pinks, and chalky whites, are marked off with ornamental ironwork and by garden walls crowded over with crape myrtle and glossy green magnolias. This scheme of squares was based on a sketch in *Villas of the Ancients* by Robert Castell, who died in an English debtors' prison—a punishment that the colony of Georgia was founded expressly to alleviate.

# The Anderson House

The Anderson House, on the corner of its square, is part of the Savannah scene. It is a family home of extraordinary personality: those black Napoleonic doors in the dining room, with that ornamented cornice, the old family furniture, mostly Empire, and the family portraits looking on.

*Stoller*

In the drawing room, with its lofty ceiling, the Empire chaise sets the tone, but the important piece is the cane-seated armchair that belonged to Thomas Jefferson.

# THE EARLIEST AND OTHER MASSACHUSETTS HOUSES

The John Whipple House in Ipswich

The framing is fantastic. In the Whipple down-stairs bedroom, below, the 1640 part, the cross-beam called the "summer," could almost carry a cathedral. Fortunately, the furnishings follow along from family to family. The eighteenth-century field bed, with its fish-net canopy, has a cross-and-crown coverlet woven in 1750. In the 1670 kitchen, lower left, the timbers are still extraordinary. The advent of brickmaking is indicated by the masonry of the fireplace. The seventeenth-century identity of the house is disclosed in the Elizabethan overhangs and diamond-paned windows.

*Fowler*

*Pratt*

## The Langdon Warner Hou

Now very much at home on the out-skirts of Ipswich, this house was moved here from Newburyport, ten miles away, adding its newer overhangs and semi-enclosed staircase to the town's seventeenth-century aspect.

# The Robert Paine, Jr., House

Built by his father in 1652, this house became a wedding present to the son after his graduation from Harvard in the class of 1656. (That's right, 1656.) The long room, below, was once bedroom, kitchen, and storeroom.

*Pratt*

*Fowler*

# IN AND OUT OF SANDWICH

*Pratt*

Sandwich houses range in size from the tiny "one-quarter capes" to what might be called the "full capes" or "Captain's houses." "Half-a-capes" were two windows wide, with a chimney at the end, waiting for additions.

113

*Pratt*

# Mrs. Cook's Captain's House

This house was built in 1730, on one of the town's highest knolls. The dining-room chairs are eighteenth-century Hepplewhite by Goddard of Newport, the glass drake, quite naturally, is Sandwich; as are the few pieces in the guest bedroom, lower right, with its wide inside shutters and maple four-posters.

## Colorful Quail Hollow

Since Thomas Tobey built this house in 1724, painted shingle walls have begun to supersede the weathered ones. White ones have trim of green, steel blue, or grey. Others are new, pale green, grey, or yellow, as here.

116

The old painted paneling meets up with modern wallpapers in both bedroom and dining room.

The heirloom piano, petit-point rocker, and Terry clock team up in the parlor.

*Fowler*

## AROUND BOSTON

*Stoller*

## The Old Heath House in Brookline

Heath House is full of things that have been there since it was built in 1791. In the library, below, the English bookcase has always stood there; the game of draughts is the one the selectmen of Brookline played when the house was new and Brookline a village.

In the keeping room, where things were kept, the child's chair has been in the family for three hundred years.

In the bedroom over the library, the dish-top table is Queen Anne, as is the tall-backed chair, made by Joseph Short of Newburyport when the house was new. The spread is linsey-woolsey.

119

*Pratt*

## Gore Place in Waltham

It is thought that, during his long stay in London as American *chargé d'affaires*, Christopher Gore got the plans for this house from Sir John Soane, the celebrated English architect. It has the Soane look, and it was built in 1804, while Gore was still in London. When Gore was elected Governor in 1809, seventy-five friends arrived on horseback for breakfast to celebrate. That was like Soane, as well as Gore.

Over the pedestal mahogany banquet table in the great elliptical state dining room, above, with its American Queen Anne chairs, hangs a chandelier that once belonged to Daniel Webster, who read law in Gore's office. The drawing room, right, occupies the whole end of the right-hand wing. The Governor had his private study off the big bedroom, left, with its Adam four-poster and many pieces that belonged to his family.

121

*Fowler*

## Jeremiah Lee Mansion

*Pratt*

Erected in Marblehead in 1768, for Colonel Lee, probably by his brother Captain Samuel Lee as architect-builder, the design of this mansion was undoubtedly taken from English models. Special features are the hand-painted papers in the drawing room, made to order in England; the winter kitchen, above; and the six Hepplewhite chairs, once owned by John Hancock, in the dining room.

The east drawing room, looking into the hallway below; the more simply paneled dining room, above.

# SALEM

These capacious, foursquare houses, beautifully carried out in the fashion of the Federal period, line both sides of one long block of Chestnut Street. They reflect the influence of Samuel McIntire of Salem, the finest woodcarving architect this country has ever produced.

# Samuel McIntire in Salem

McIntire was born in Salem in 1757, and died there is 1811, having lived there all his life. Contemporaries considered the mansion he built in 1802, for the merchant prince Elias H. Derby, his finest achievement. It stood on Essex Street near the Pingree house, but was torn down six years after McIntire's death. In addition to his houses, he did some of Salem's finest public buildings, of which only Assembly Hall and Hamilton Hall remain. In 1792, he submitted competitive plans for the Capitol in Washington, but William Thornton won President Washington's approval.

As with the west parlor, the east parlor has been refurnished to an earlier period since this picture was taken. However it is furnished it will always be one of McIntire's most triumphant Adam rooms.

*Pratt*

# The Pingree House

The late Victorian paint seen here has now been removed from the façade, exposing its original, delicate pink brick. The so-called marriage bed below is a Salem bed of around 1800, and the secretary is attributed to William Appleton, a Salem Federal cabinetmaker.

*Fowler*

Marvelously framed sliding doors separate the two parlors to the right of the main entrance. In the parlor through the door, the wallpaper panels are French; the furniture is Salem Federal; and the rug is a very delicate Aubusson. The piano is a Benjamin Crehore. The painting above is a portrait of Esther (Gerrish) Carpenter, 1751-94, of Salem. The dining room is below on the left, and on the right is the Shaw bedroom, with Shaw family Federal pieces.

# Cogswell's Grant at Essex

The grant was given to John Cogswell in 1634, by the town of Ipswich. A Cogswell built the house in the late 1700's and painted it this mellow pumpkin color. A Mr. Boyd bought it in 1839, raised acres of peacocks, and sold the meat in Boston for $1.00 a pound.

*Stoller*

132

A rarity itself, the house is full of rarities. The parlor is opposite, the living room above, and a bedroom to the right. The woodwork finish, such as the superb graining in the bedroom, is a feature of the house, as are the floor coverings throughout.

# NANTUCKET AND THE VINEYARD

Martha's Vineyard was settled in 1642, Nantucket in 1659. The Vineyard has about 250 square miles, Nantucket a little more than 50. The Vineyard is six miles by ferry from Woods Hole on the Cape, Nantucket twenty. The settlers began with fishing and farming. They then went in for whaling, got rich, and built lovely houses. Then whaling went out. Now the islands are summer resorts, their populations decimated in winter. The town of Nantucket, and the town of Edgartown on the Vineyard, are remarkably harmonious, as has been noticed by visitors as far apart as Crevecoeur in the 1780's and the late Talbot Hamlin in recent years; visual harmony is an island characteristic. In the early days, the Islanders (the Nantucketeers especially) brought their building lumber, even their firewood, by packet from as far away as Maine, just as they do today from the Massachusetts mainland. The remarkable Crevecoeur wrote of a habit of the whalers' wives: "A singular custom prevails here among the women at which I was greatly surprised . . . they have adopted these many years the Asiatic custom of taking a taste of opium every morning; and so deeply rooted is it that they would be at a loss to live without this indulgence." And not only the women. The sheriff, he said, "takes three grains a day after breakfast, without which he would be unable to conduct his affairs." Be that as it may, we are now to see the kind of houses the whaling barons built, beginning with the Three Bricks on Main Street, Nantucket—West Brick, Middle Brick, and East Brick—built, identically, in 1838, by Joseph Starbuck, a whaling fleet owner, for each of his three sons.

# Three Bricks

*Stoller*

One way to see what the whaling fleet owners were like is to take a look at the way they lived. An East Brick bedroom is shown on the left, the big double drawing room is below, and the library is on the right below. The bedroom's massive mahogany four-poster is a Nantucket piece of 1812, the year the British bombarded the island. The wing-back chair in chintz in the first drawing room is also from Nantucket, and the portrait is by the teacher of Joshua Reynolds. William Starbuck ran the family whaling business from the library when his two brothers went to sea.

The house shown above the library is a captain's house a little way out of town.

# Major Josiah Coffin's House on Nantucket

The Coffins were already old-timers on the island when Josiah Coffin built this house in 1724. Grandfather Tristram had put up the first Coffin homestead, near Capuam pond. In 1686, Josiah's father, Jethro, had built his house nearby on Sunset Hill, where it still stands—the oldest surviving house on the island. Not a trace remains of Tristram's. It may have been pried apart and transported in sections back to the Massachusetts mainland. This happened to several hundred old Nantucket houses in the early 1800's when the long-prosperous whaling industry suffered a depression.

The furniture of the southwest bedroom is virtually all from the island. The Japanese prints were brought in during the China-trade days. The chair on the left-hand side of the fireplace is a fine old brace-back, fanback Windsor.

# The Captain's House in Edgartown

Captain Jared Fisher was the whaling captain for whom the house was built in 1832. It faces the harbor at Edgartown, now a summer resort. The whaling bark *Canton* was one of the captain's commands; during her whaling days the *Canton* made more than $2,000,000 from whalebone and oil for her several owners. The Austrian paper in the long dining room, right, is hand-painted in panels, with the New York harbor over the fine Philadelphia sideboard and the Philadelphia waterworks over the mantelpiece.

That is Captain Fisher's gold-headed cane in the newel of the staircase, and through the doorway is Edgartown Harbor.

The portrait in this nautical front parlor is of Captain Fisher's father-in-law, Captain John Osborn. The model on the mantel is the *Canton*.

All the pictures, quilts, rugs, samplers, and upholstery in the master bedroom are either hand-sewn or embroidered.

# FROM PORTSMOUTH WEST TO SHELBURNE AND THE SHAKERS

## Then Down East to Kittery, Portland, Rockport and Columbia Falls

While Maine was still a province of Massachusetts, and Vermont still seeking statehood, and western Massachusetts was very much under the influence of New York, Portsmouth on the Piscataqua, with its own waterway to the sea, was the great landway to this whole west and northwest region and to the down-east coastline to Canada. As a city it is still the finest repository of splendid old houses north of Salem. Shelburne, in western Vermont, separated from New York by Lake Champlain, is a repository of quite another sort, a kind of historical microcosm of the state, a collector's paradise. Scattered along the western fringe of New England are hamlets of the Shakers, the eastern traces of these last settlements of a sect whose furniture and other artifacts are choice examples, more and more rare, of American cult culture. Finally, the four Maine-Coast houses here constitute four chapters in the history of this fabulous shoreline.

In the Rundlet-May drawing room, the pink, figured wallpaper, with its daisy border, is the original, as are the knight's-lance curtain poles. The young lady is Louisa Catherine Rundlet May, daughter of James and Jane Rundlet, and one of their thirteen children who grew up here.

# Portsmouth Mansion

Or "Manshon House," as James Rundlet called it in his account books. The first purchase was of 7,146 feet of boards and planks, $75.00. In April, 1807, William Tucker got $7.20 for "blowing rock." By September, the joiners were in. Their board alone was $212.50. And what's this! —"45 gallons of rum for workmen this past summer —$45.00." Jane and James Rundlet moved in in May, 1809. They had already bought the big four-poster —$21.00.

In the parlor, the pair of Hepplewhite love seats is priceless. On the marble mantelpiece is the double silhouette of Jane and James.

*Stoller*

# The Dutton House

Salmon Dutton built the house in 1782, in the town of Cavendish, Vermont, a hundred miles southeast of Shelburne Village. It was J. Watson Webb and the late Mrs. Webb who brought it to Shelburne as part of their rare community museum near Lake Champlain, from whose waters the Webbs also brought the old sidewheeler *Ticonderoga* to keep company with the old country stores and endless other items of Vermontiana.

Between the Queen Anne highboy and the painted pine four-poster stands a wonderful high-back Windsor.

In the Dutton dining room the two prize features are the stenciled wall decorations and the painted highboy.

Outstanding in the Dutton parlor are the rush-bottomed ladder-back chair, the stenciling, as in the dining room, and the primitive portrait.

*Stoller*

148

*Stoller*

## Shaker House

In this old house in the Shaker community around Richmond, Massachusetts, near the New York State line, the Shaker authorities Mr. and Mrs. E. D. Andrews recreated an authentic Shaker dwelling, concentrating on the purity and perfectionism of Shaker craftsmanship. The floors are Shaker red, and everything is Shaker-made: the living-room stove, the candelabra and the carpeting.

150

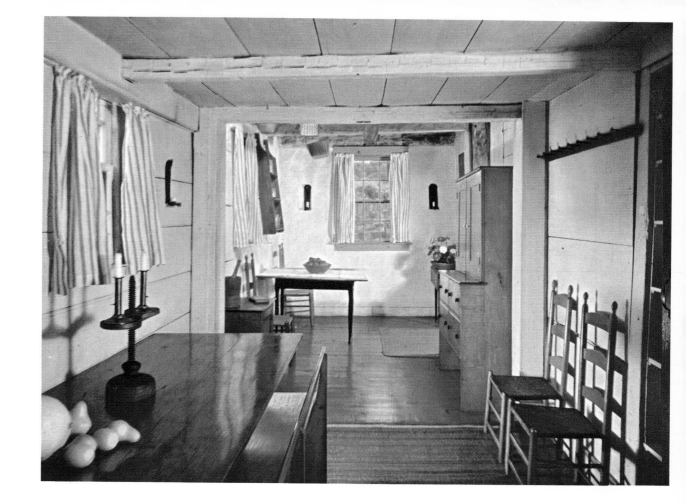

Running the length of the house in back is the old weaving room, now a dining and breakfast room.

Honest craftsmanship was part of the Shaker creed, including kitchen utensils: the soapstone sink here on its wooden stand, and the tables and counters.

151

# MAINE

The four houses here are all within smelling distance of the sea: the Lady Pepperrell House at Kittery, across the Piscataqua from Portsmouth, where the coast of Maine begins; the Tate at Portland, fifty miles farther along; Spite House at Rockport, a headland out from Camden; and the Ruggles at Columbia Falls, about seventy miles from the Canadian border at Calais (pronounced "callous"). Route 1 is the the road to take the whole way, and either spring or fall is the best time to take it. Of these four houses, all but Spite House are open to the public. Pictured on the opposite page, Spite House was built by young Captain Thomas McCobb, grown rich with his trading fleet. The Lady Pepperrell was built for Lady Pepperrell herself, whose husband Sir William, who had died the year before she began, was born rich at Kittery Point nearby, and became the first native American to be knighted by the Crown. The Tate's builder, George Tate, came to Falmouth in 1775, as Mast Agent for the London Syndicate, and began to build his house the moment he arrived. Lastly, it took Thomas Ruggles from Massachusetts twenty years to make his fortune in timber and build, in 1816, that gem of a house of his in Columbia Falls. The widow of a titled American military man; a successful sea trader; a key man in England's naval lifeline; and a self-made timber baron—together they constitute a cross section of the upper crust of Maine before and after the Revolution.

# Spite House

Spite House came by its name because Captain McCobb, when he built it, wanted to get back at his widowed stepmother, who lived across the street in a house that until then was acclaimed as the finest in all that part of Maine. That was in Phippsburg Center, down the Kennebec from Bath, in 1806. Then in 1925, Spite house caught the eye of a connoisseur, who had it loaded bodily on a pair of barges and towed eighty miles up the coast to a wooded knoll on Deadman's Point at Rockport. As someone once said of another such undertaking, "What God could do if He only had the dough." But more impressive than the moving operation is the way the new owners made the old house look so elegantly at home in its new surroundings.

*Pratt*

*Stoller*

Transplanted Spite House, above, and its transformed drawing room below.

The Spite House dining-room carpet and cornice are *tours de force* of reproduction.

A rare Maine mantel and chest of pumpkin pine are features of this bedroom.

# The Lady Pepperrell Mansion

What Lady Pepperrell was like has not been recorded, but her house is very *grande dame,* and it has been said of her that even after the Revolution rendered her title null and void, she demanded the deference she still fancied to be her due.

The dining-room table is by Duncan Phyfe, the floor, painted.

The table, with its tea chest under the Chippendale mirror in the Lady Pepperrell parlor, is also by Duncan Phyfe. The portrait above the mantelpiece, which, with the cornice, carries out the elegance of the front façade, is Sir William's youngest sister Jane.

*Stoller*

# The Tate House—Portland, 1775

The rare raised attic (for the slaves), the extra slim siding, and the nicely set windows tell a lot about Captain Tate. Outside it is a New Englander's house; but it is a Londoner's within, as the dining and stair hall shown below indicate. It is only a surmise, but a fashionable shipwright, familiar with both sides of the ocean, must have been the inevitable builder-craftsman in charge here.

The west bedroom of the Tate House has a cupboard in the paneling for wigs, and a bedspread of copperplate print.

*Stoller*

## The Ruggles House

The house now stands close up to the street in Columbia Falls, which still has the earmarks of the timber town of 1818. The building of the house was in the hands of a woodcarving carpenter whose name should not have been forgotten. There are only legends about him, but they are nice ones: that an angel guided his hand, and that he had worked in London for the brothers Adam. Thomas Ruggles had only two years' time to enjoy his house; he died in 1820.

The handcarving on the drawing room mantelpiece, right, in cherrywood on white with columned corners, is one of the minor wonders of Maine.

The hallway, left, is a dramatic sight with this masterpiece of a divided staircase flying up to the floor above.

161

# NEWPORT
# AND
# PROVIDENCE

These cities were joint capitals of tiny Rhode Island until 1900. Politically, in the early days, Newport was the patrician capital, Providence the plebeian and at times in the past the rivalry between them was intense. Now Newport rests on its laurels, and Providence proceeds apace. Newport's great period was that of the Nichols house. The Providence houses date from the substantial Providence fortunes of the early Republic. The old sections of both cities are oases of gracious and stylish building.

# Newport's Nichols

It is known as the Nichols-Wanton-Hunter house. Nichols built it in 1746, but it was Joseph Wanton, Jr., who bought it ten years later and built into it the beauty that distinguished it today. At the outbreak of the Revolution, the house became the very handsome headquarters of Admiral de Ternay, commanding the French fleet based in the harbor to keep the British away. After that, Dr. William Hunter had the house until he died in 1849. The Preservation Society of Newport County is to be credited for the whole job of restoration here, and elsewhere in the town.

*Stoller*

The dining-room paneling, left, is finished in rose cedar graining. The Newport notables are the Reverend John Callender, and, in the hall, Captain John Brown.

Designed to be an upstairs parlor, the room above became de Ternay's bedroom, and in it he died. The superb paneling, particularly of the fireplace wall, with its shell cupboards on either side, are of real parlor importance. Gilbert Stuart's portrait of Mrs. John Banister and her daughter hangs above a priceless Newport desk.

# The Nightingale-Brown

Caleb Ormsbee designed this house, and Joseph Nightingale built it in 1792. Most recently it has been the home of John Nicholas Brown, whose family has been one to conjure with in Providence since before the Revolution. The house, with its tall, pedimented Palladian front, stands at the top of the hill that dominates the city. Its palatial scale and character are reflected in the magnificent drawing room, below, which contains some of the richest examples of late eighteenth-century woodwork in the United States.

*Stoller*

With its damask walls, and queenly canopied four-poster, this must be the biggest bedroom in early America.

## The Eliza Brown Ward House

Mrs. Ward, who built this in 1813, was the daughter of Joseph Brown, an early amateur architect of Providence. It was from Brown that Caleb Ormsbee obtained a copy of James Gibbs' *Book of Architecture*, which provided the inspiration for the Nightingale façade. But who designed the Ward house situated on the side of a hill, is not yet known. The spectacular feature of the adjoining parlor and drawing room on the opposite page is, naturally, the wallpapers. They were installed soon after the house was built and just after they were first printed. They are both from the factory of Joseph Dufour in Paris. That in the far room is the "Bank of the Bosphorus," of 1816, composed of landscapes with river and caiques, and consisting of twenty-four strips. That in the near room is commonly known as "Pizzaro in Peru," thirty strips, and based on Pizzaro's invasion of 1531—a mad, beautiful, and savage melee, as romantically depicted here.

The dining-room walls are covered with Chinese tea papers. The portrait is of the present owner's great-grandmother, who rocked the cradle in the corner.

# The Carrington House

Captain Edward Carrington, merchant, shipowner, shipbuilder, and for a while Consul at Canton, bought this brownstone mansion two years after it was built in 1810. He added a third story and the tier of porches. Many of the furnishings in the great connecting drawing rooms reflect the Captain's close attachment to the China trade and also the colorful taste of those robust times.

The scale of the four-poster dwarfs even the big highboy.

Porcelains and Chinese chairs flank the double-framed doorway.

# CONNECTICUT

Connecticut sparkles all over with antique towns, like a house full of heirlooms. If it weren't for Massachusetts, it would have more communities dating from the 1600's than any other State, all well-kept and lovely to look at, with Litchfield very likely in the lead in that respect, the parlor town *par excellence*. Wethersfield has the history, and Stonington the charm, but Litchfield has the queenly quality that it takes: one long elm-lined avenue bordered by house after house of true distinction. None is more distinguished than the one called Sheldon's Tavern, at the right. It was somewhat simple-looking when Elisha Sheldon built it in 1760, and remained so when Sheldon's son turned it into a tavern twenty years later. Then, about 1800, it was worked upon by a talented Connecticut craftsman-architect named William Spratt, who gave it the columns, the Palladian window, and the pediment above. He reworked the cornices, corniced the first floor windows, and set a balustrade upon the roof. All these improvements were made too late for Washington to have seen them when he passed the night in the tavern on his way back from Wethersfield.

Washington only passed through. Ethan Allen was born here, and so were Harriet Beecher Stowe and Henry Ward Beecher, her brother.

Litchfield is in the western highlands of the state. In the eastern highlands is the town of Coventry, where Nathan Hale was born, and where the house built by his father just before his death is preserved. In between the two highlands runs the Connecticut River, in whose broad valley early Connecticut history was made. Suffield, up near the Massachusetts border, with Hastings Hill; Farmington, back of Hartford, with the two Cowles houses; Wethersfield with the Webb; Millington Society, farther down the river, with the Mowings; and East Haddam with Dunstaffnage are all beautiful. Then there are the houses along the coast line on Long Island Sound, from Darien, with Bonnet Hill; Fairfield, with the old Ogden saltbox; and finally the Stonington uplands, with Stonecrop, the Denison family house, and Anguilla.

## Farmington

In the valley country west of Hartford, settled in 1640, Farmington is also a parlor town, with some fine Federal streets, beautiful fences, and Miss Porter's School for girls (1843). The two Cowles houses are a special attraction. This one with the nice porch, built in 1782, belonged to the father, General Solomon Cowles; it is now the home of the Horace Walpole specialist Wilmarth Lewis. One of its special attractions is the fireplace wall of the drawing room, opposite.

Queen for a

This is the finest woodwork in Connecticut, outstanding for the richness of its detail, the robustness of its carving.

# The George Cowles House in Farmington

The son's house, built in 1804, was a wedding present from his father the General. It is thought to be the work of the same William Spratt who worked on Sheldon's Tavern, and probably did other Connecticut houses similar in scale. Its main features are the Classical portico surmounting the arcaded basement loggia, and the spectacular staircase leading to the third floor, where the ballroom used to be.

The dining-room sideboard is English Hepplewhite, and the painting above it is a notable example of its period, called "Coursing in Sussex," by James Ward, R.A. The pastoral scene above the mantel is a van der Meulen.

## Hastings Hill in Suffield

This is the private restoration of a perfectionist. The color outside matches the color Hastings Hill was painted in 1737, and the woodwork inside has the polish and glow of a Stradivarius. The living room, opposite, below, is sheathed on the fireplace wall with feather-edged pine boards which, most unusually, run horizontally. The decorated Connecticut chest is the prize of the bedroom, above; the feather-crested bannister-back chair and the dignified "necessary" chair, both early eighteenth century, like the house, are also prizes.

The slate-green living room, above, is more formally paneled than the other rooms. The chair (left) is a bannister back with pierced crest; the chalk pigeons are from Pennsylvania.

*Pratt*

## The Nathan Hale House

Hale, a young schoolteacher recently out of Yale, saw the house go up, but died the same year his father finished it, in 1776, when he was captured behind the British lines and hanged as a spy. The pewter in the dining room, above, belonged to the patriot's sister Joanna. The old pine table is one at which Washington ate breakfast at nearby Brigham Tavern.

The blanket chest is a Hale heirloom; the cornice piece an oddity.

The armchair (left) and wing chair, in the parlor, below, are country Chippendale.

# The Mowings

The Mowings is a late seventeenth-century farmhouse in a once prosperous sawmill community known as Millington Society, far away in a woods filled with pheasant and deer and centered on the town of East Haddam.

*Pratt*

The dining table came from an ancient country cheese factory in Vermont; the trencher table in the corner, from an old New England tavern.

A Mowings ancestor in 1799 watched Washington's
funeral from this rocking chair.

Throughout, the marvel of the house is the color
and patina of the old pine.

181

*Pratt*

# Dunstaffnage at East Haddam

Dunstaffnage was built in 1738, by a blacksmith from Massachusetts who came to East Haddam and married a land-rich widow. It stayed in the family until 1880, then went through fifty years of hard times, from which it was lucky enough to be rescued by an architect-archeologist whose handiwork is beautifully apparent. In the living room, below, the 1750 highboy is prized almost as much as the entirely original Erastus Hughes clock over the old granite fireplace.

*Fowler*

The dining room was remodeled for a bride of the house in 1790. The detail of the mantel and corner post is immaculate. The owner has reason to believe that the Parthenon mirror may have been made for Monticello.

# Bonnet Hill at Darien

Bonnet Hill boasts a living room with four paneled
walls—extremely rare in Connecticut. The house was
built before 1700, in Stamford, became a millinery shop
in the 1850's, and then moved to Darien, in the 1950's.

184

Pumpkin yellow and oyster white, right, was a favorite primitive color scheme. The bedroom, above, and dining room, below, are also done in old colors; the latter with sour milk, egg white, and iron-rust paint.

The living room began as the lean-to kitchen; its huge fireplace is still lined with the old cooking implements.

# The Ogden at Fairfield

Fairfield was settled in 1641, and a man named Ogden built this saltbox a little way outside the settlement in 1690. This short distance from town saved the life of the house in the Revolution, when the British landed, burned most of Fairfield, and hurried on to Danbury. Thus the Ogden saltbox is the oldest house in Fairfield, a historic Connecticut town. Many noteworthy Georgian houses are located at nearby Southport on the Sound.

*Stoller*

Early Primitives decorate the walls of the principal bedroom, and a Chippendale child's chair stands by the fireplace.

Pratt

# The Webb House

When Joseph Webb set about building his house in 1752, his carpenters and joiners went ahead in true Connecticut style. No craftsmen in the colonies could build as well in wood as the ones in Connecticut, where practice made perfect. The Webb house exhibits unusually well the virtuosity of the Connecticut woodworking craftsmen, who not only wanted their work to look right, but to last forever, and to stay tight, firm, and straight. No cracks, no creaking on the stairs, no partings in the paneling were to be allowed. Inside, this is all made clear in the three principal rooms: the parlor, above, the dining room, left, and the famous bedroom on the following page. In these rooms one of the most momentous events of the whole Revolutionary War occurred in 1781: Washington elected to meet here with Rochambeau to work out a way to victory—a victory that came less than five months later. Washington arrived on May 19, and stayed until May 24. Rochambeau reached here from Newport on May 20, and returned on May 23. Washington used the bedroom with the famous French red flocked wallpaper. In his diary he put down, "24th. Set out on my return—dined at Farmington and lodged at Litchfield." That was his night at Sheldon's Tavern.

This is where Washington slept, and that is the red flocked wallpaper on the far wall.

*Pratt*

# Stonington Upland

Stonington extends for five miles from the Mystic to the Paw-
catuck, and takes in several widely separated towns, including
Mystic. The Denison Homestead stands up the hill from Mystic
on its great granite boulders. Stonecrop, above, and Anguilla are
in the hills above Stonington Village, which has to be seen to be
believed. The territory was settled in 1649, probably first by
Elisha Cheseborough and his family, who built his house on a
knoll at the head of Wequetequock Cove. The house was burned
in 1707, and was rebuilt into Anguilla.

It seems that in 1717, George Denison III built
a new, larger house for Lucy Gallup, his pretty bride,
on the site of his grandfather's "grate manor house"
at Pequot-sepes. Eleven generations have since lived
in the "new" house, and it has now been preserved
to reflect the various periods of occupancy, from the
eighteenth-century bedroom, above, and kitchen,
right, to post-Victorian days.

## The Denison Homestead

*Stoller*

# Anguilla

When the 1660 Cheseborough house burned in 1707, this much larger house was built with what could be used of the ruins. Its size and stylishness make it outstanding for that early date.

This bedroom, like the dining room opposite, is a full twenty feet square. Each room is spanned by two summer beams instead of the usual one. The two fireplaces could have been in the original 1660 chimney.

In both rooms, most of the early furniture that was there when these photographs were taken is American Queen Anne. The woodwork of the paneled walls is part of the 1770 rebuilding.

# NEW YORK, PENNSYLVANIA,

# NEW JERSEY AND DELAWARE

Of course, Connecticut also could have been called a river colony, because of the settlements that were made up the Connecticut and lesser rivers along the Sound. But Connecticut overland migrations from Massachusetts and Rhode Island figured importantly. Whereas the center point of New York Harbor and the penetration of the Hudson River were the primary means of settlement here from early Dutch days till after the Revolution, the same could be said of what the Delaware did for the colonies of Pennsylvania, New Jersey and Delaware itself. First the Dutch and the Swedes, and finally, with finality, the English, whose houses tell the history of these three Delaware-fed colonies, all managed at crucial points by the ministrations of William Penn and his people.

# Rock Hall at Lawrence

Josiah Martin, an Englishman from Antigua, bought 600 acres of farmland, now the town of Lawrence, Long Island, and in 1767, built Rock Hall. In 1787, he left the property to his son Samuel, a Loyalist, who was under bond during the Revolution "to behave peacibly." Samuel Martin lived well, kept nine slaves, and gave Rock Hall a reputation for hospitality. After his death, the estate went from bad to worse until Thomas Hewlett bought it in 1824, and put it back into shape. It was kept that way by his descendants, who presented it in 1948, with three acres of land, to the Town of Hempstead. A bedroom and a parlor are opposite, the dining and drawing rooms appear on the next page.

The drawing room has been kept as
stylish as the house itself, powder-white
as a wig in its nicely landscaped little
park, and filled with finery. This is one
of a pair of rooms which were redone
in the Federal fashion around 1800,
presumably for a great family gathering.

The dining room woodwork looks as it did when the house was new. The dining room is now furnished in American Chippendale, with a fine Chinese rug on the floor. Delft tiles frame the fireplace, and some beautiful pieces of porcelain fill the wall cabinet. Although it is in Lawrence, the house is a museum of the Town of Hempstead, which can be proud of what it has done and is doing here.

In the House of History drawing room, the secretary is New York State Chippendale; all the rest is by Duncan Phyfe. The four-poster in the bedroom is a fine Hudson Valley piece.

The portrait on the drawing room mantel, left, is of Major Mordecai Myers, second owner of the house. Myers bought it in 1836, from Judge Van der Poel, who had built it in 1810, using the skill of a gifted architect-carpenter named Barnabas Waterman. It is a tribute in the Federal style to the great architectural tradition of the Hudson River Valley, with old house after old house, from the mansions of the early Dutch-English patricians, to Huguenot villages, and to Victorian castles of incredible luxury.

*Andrews*

# The House of History

The dining room is the finest feature of the house.

*Stoller*

# The Thompson House in Setauket

The Thompson House dates from shortly before 1720, with a weathered silver exterior, and glowing indoors with the color and patina that only age and wear can give to oak framing and pine paneling. In these circumstances austerity is transformed. To visit the house is a stirring experience.

# The Jayne House

This house was built a little *after* 1720, and a few miles away from the Thompson House at East Setauket. It was built by William Jayne, a chaplain in Cromwell's army and an Oxford graduate, who fled here when Charles II took the throne. The most outstanding feature of this house is the freehand paintings on the walls. Mr. Howard G. Sherwood was the saviour and preserver of the house, and the donor.

*Stoller*

# Ganset House in East Hampton

Out toward the end of Long Island, the natives think nothing of lifting up one of the early frame houses and putting it down somewhere else. The houses are framed with such strength and stiffness that they take it all in their stride. Ganset House was one. It was built about 1700, in Amagansett, where it got its name, and was moved a couple of centuries later to East Hampton, a matter of a few miles. It stands there now as though nothing had ever happened to it.

*Stoller*

Naturally, there is nice pine paneling; in the living room, on the left, and in the bedroom, above, and the dining room, below. But what stands out is the positively dramatic framing; the oversize hand-hewn beams of iron-hard oak spell power and performance. If it is like framing in Connecticut, there just may be a reason. This end of Long Island was once a part of that colony across Long Island Sound.

*Stoller*

Pratt

# Home Sweet Home

Built in the very early 1700's, this house was bought, a hundred years later, by some people named Payne. Then in 1823, an opera produced in London, called *Clari, or the Maid of Milan,* contained the song that has been sung ever since. As the words were written by John Howard Payne, of the East Hampton Paynes, it didn't take long for the title of the song to be given to the house.

All the rooms are furnished in the various periods of the Payne family ownership, and on the paneled wall of the parlor is a portrait of the poet.

207

# PENNSYLVANIA

## One of the Prides of Philadelphia

Back in colonial days, and on after the Revolution, the hills above both banks of the winding Schuylkill were ideal for country seats and summer homes. The region has long been devotedly preserved as one of the largest and finest city parks in the country, and the old mansions that adorn its little hills are protected and maintained in the Park forever.

Of all the houses in the Park, Mount Pleasant is the most imposing, for John Macpherson, who built it in 1761, was lavish with the money he made from privateering, and expense was no object. Then, too, Philadelphia artisans were men of extraordinary taste and talent, and the house inside and out is a monument to their skill—boldly conceived and brilliantly executed. Few colonial façades were as richly designed as that of Mount Pleasant, with its brickwork quoins and its Palladian window above its bold Tuscan doorway. In 1779, it passed from Macpherson to Major General Benedict Arnold, at that time the American commander at Philadelphia. Arnold bought it for his bride, the famous beauty Peggy Shippen. Fate, however, had other things in store for him and he never had a chance to occupy it. Like most of the Park mansions, Mount Pleasant is open to the public.

# Andalusia and Other Aspects of Bucks County

Bucks County is not just a county; it is a phenomenon. Filled from New Hope north with refugees from Manhattan, and from New Hope south with commuters from Philadelphia, it still looks as it has for the past 250 years. Farmers are still farming the same fields, the towns are still the same. The stone houses that the city people buy don't change easily. The big stone barns still contain crops and cows, and the same country stores carry on at the crossroads. Turnpikes miraculously just miss it, and vast housing developments so far haven't disfigured it. It has harbored more than its share of famous painters, playwrights, poets, humorists, and best-selling novelists, and has taken them in its stride. The county has always taken everything in its stride—including its biggest early house, called Andalusia. The county hardly knows the house is there. This great house is in the lowest corner of the county, safe in its own private park, a glorious Greek temple of a house, looking out across the lordly Delaware, and still beautifully lived in by the same Biddle family whose Nicholas Biddle built it in the 1830's. This was *the* Biddle, the most famous financier of his day; statesman, scholar, editor, and connoisseur, he was one of our earliest travelers to the Greek ruins of Italy and Athens. Thomas U. Walter was his architect, but it was Biddle who spelled out the Doric Temple of Poseidon at Paestum, making this the most distinguished dwelling of the Greek Revival in America.

One of the two yellow drawing rooms at Andalusia, glowing with gilt and decorated with Greek details of the period on all the woodwork.

The bookcases, painted with Classical decoration of the period, and the elegant old fruitwood sofa are features of the Biddle library at Andalusia.

The marble mantel of the music room is Italian; most of the furniture is French Empire.

## New Hope on the Delaware

Far up the river from Andalusia, this old town has
become Bucks County's favorite rendezvous. There are
countless visitors to its theaters, restaurants, shops,
bistros, and galleries. Indestructibly attractive, it is not
only decorated by the Delaware and by its old streets
and houses, but also by the old Pennsylvania Canal,
whose principal purpose now is to be picturesque—like
some of the citizens.

An unusually good example of the Bucks County white-plastered stone house, this one has four distinct roof levels in line, denoting different steps of construction. It is in the lower part of the county.

In the very best Bucks County tradition, this fine old farmhouse in the upper part of the county, in a place called Pleasant Valley, has been restored with the taste and respect it commands. Both the house and its immense barn are all of "tailored" stone.

The farther up the county one goes, the more colorful the barns become. Red is the favorite color, but there are plenty of yellows and pale greens; all have hex signs decorating their wooden walls to ward off ill fortune.

## Ingham Manor at Aquetong

This mellow old manor is marked by manor-house touches in the flat-arched heads of its doors and windows, as well as in the fineness of its masonry of "tailored-stone," as the county people call it. It dates from about 1750, but much later houses could look the same, since Bucks County stone house style was very stable. This manor house is a mile or two from New Hope on the road to Doylestown, the county seat.

Another fine old manor house, near Mechanicsville, has been beautifully restored, as these pictures make plain. They show, too, that bold colors and Empire furniture are often better backgrounds for today than period perfectionism.

218

*Pratt*

The barn above has typical Bucks County bigness and beauty,
the house it belongs to, a very special stateliness along with its
distinguished stonework.

219

*Pratt*

Nobody built better in Bucks County than the Quakers, and the meeting houses of the Friends are models of beautiful masonry and generous proportions. This is the famous Solebury meeting house, in a delightful country community in the hills not far above New Hope.

Pratt

# Valley Forge

In the valley of the Schuylkill, twenty-odd miles from Bucks County, Isaac Potts, son of John Potts of Pottsgrove, and an ironmaster like his father and his father's father, built this house fifteen miles from Pottsgrove, in 1758. In December, 1777, he turned it over to General Washington. The house was so crowded that the General had a log cabin built as a dining room for him and his officers, with whom he made a practice of sharing his meals. The evening before his birthday, Martha Washington came to join her husband. They stayed together at Valley Forge until June, keeping up the courage of the men during those desperate days. Isaac Potts brought his family back after the Revolution, and lived here until he died in 1805.

The initials "I.P." are engraved in the 1775 walnut desk in the parlor. Like the Philadelphia Chippendale chairs, the furniture is all from Pennsylvania.

In Martha's bedroom, the officers' and neighbors' wives gathered daily to knit and patch for the soldiers.

*Balz*

The Potts's kitchen, with the customary brick floor and the equally customary cavern of a fireplace.

## Pottsgrove

One of the great prides of Pennsylvania, this heavenly stone mansion was built near Pottstown in 1752, by the famous ironmaster, John Potts, who reared a family of thirteen and died here in 1768. His son Thomas inherited the house, and all through the Revolution, Washington, a friend of the family, made it a convenient meeting place for himself and his generals.

As in the dining room, above, and the bedroom, right, the woodwork is in keeping with the vigor, boldness, and beauty of the house itself.

Through the doorway of the children's dining room, opposite, can be seen the miller's house, part of the original Pottsgrove property. The chest is Pennsylvania Dutch, the burl bowl, early Pennsylvania.

The bedroom, above left, is the one Washington occupied; the portrait over the parlor mantel is of the Washington family, relaxed as they were during their Germantown sojourn. The handsome secretary desk there is from New England. In the dining room, opposite, the Hepplewhite chairs and the Philadelphia Hepplewhite cabinet belonged to the Morris family, as did the set of Chinese export porcelain.

# The Deshler-Morris House

This house on Market Square in Germantown was built in 1772 by David Deshler, a dabbler in pharmacy, whose salve is still being sold. After the battle of Germantown, Sir William Howe, the British commander, spent a few weeks there. During most of the summer of 1794, when Philadelphia was the capital of the new country, President Washington stayed there with his family. Robert Morris, famous as "the financier of the Revolution," then bought it and lived there until his bankruptcy.

*Stoller*

# NEW JERSEY

*Stoller*

# Holmeland in Salem County

Salem County houses like Holmeland are a connecting link between the Philadelphia town houses and the Delaware houses. In 1729, Colonel Benjamin Holme built the middle part of this house, almost across from New Castle. The wings came later. The big dining room and kitchen beyond are in the original section, and represent the realistic adaptation of early house conditions to present-day living.

# DELAWARE

## New Castle to Odessa to Dover

These, the most enchanting old towns in Delaware, are also among the most enchanting in America. Smyrna is lovely, too, where a side road leads to the house called Aspendale. New Castle is the oldest. The Swedes had it for a while, then the Dutch, then the English. Part of the handsome old court house in its ancient park was already standing in 1682, when New Castle became the capital of the territory. The streets are still quiet and serene; the waterfront street called The Strand still looks out across the wide Delaware to Salem County; and the houses are still old pink brick; the side yards, shady green.

*Pratt*

# The George Read House

George Read died before his house was finished in 1801, but it will always be the George Read House. He was a member of the Continental Congress and President of Delaware during the Revolution, and he helped make Delaware the first state to ratify the Constitution in 1789. His house still presides over The Strand. The Kinsey John, Jr., House of 1823, left, is typical of the town's unpretentious charm.

231

*Pratt*

# The Corbit-Sharp House in Odessa

This tidewater community was named after the great Ukrainian grain port because half a million bushels of wheat a year were being shipped from there to Europe, by barges down Appoquinimink Creek to big grain schooners anchored offshore in Delaware Bay. Today there isn't a sign of this golden activity; just peace, and quiet. In this nice but unspectacular town there is an absolutely beguiling cluster of colonial houses, and this one is Odessa's pride and joy. The William Corbit who built it between 1772 and 1774, was a rich Quaker tanner trained in Philadelphia. Thanks to his methodical ways, the present owners can account for everything from the granite foundation to the *chinoiserie* balustrade on the rooftop. They can also establish that Corbit brought three brides to the house, and that in it his thirteen children were born. But credit the beauty of the house to the handbooks of Abraham Swan and the artistry of its colonial carpenter, Robert May. The house was given to the Winterthur Museum, the present administrators, by H. Rodney Sharp, a later owner.

*Guerrero*

The Corbits called this upstairs drawing room the "long room." Its architecture is by Swan; its furniture came from Philadelphia.

Among other things, the library is distinguished by its wonderful woodwork, its Philadelphia Chippendale desk and bookcase, and its New England easy chair.

In the master bedroom downstairs, the bed and the chair beside it are early Philadelphia; the carpet is Irish; the paneling is by May out of Swan's handbook.

In the dining room the laurels again go to Messrs. May and Swan. The table is from Virginia, the chairs from Philadelphia. The kitchen pewter is English.

*Guerrero*

If the flavor here seems masculine, it is because this room was William Corbit's office.

All the paneling of the northeast bedroom still carries its original coat of paint. The inherited highboy and early four-poster are notable features.

A third-floor fireplace is undoubtedly the smallest in this next-to-the-smallest state. The dwarf tongs were the gift of Henry Francis duPont of Winterthur.

# Aspendale at Downs Chapel

Aspendale was built between 1771 and 1773, by Charles Numbers, the great-great-grandfather of the present owner. During the Revolution the lead was stripped from the roof to make bullets, and in Victorian times someone in the family put on a fancy verandah. But the 1773 paint on the interior woodwork is still there today. And all is pristine and pure again, inside and out.

*Stoller*

In the hallway the whole fireplace wall is paneled. The staircase door leads to the winding stairs above. The original paint was simply cleaned and waxed.

In the study the chimney breast is strongly detailed up to a sturdily molded cornice. The paint on the plaster is the same as the original lime wash.

The fireplace of the great room is flanked in its paneled wall by a pair of closed grey china cupboards on either side of the fireplace.

# The House on the Green

The old Green is Dover's lovely oasis. The fine original side of the State House faces it, but the Ridgley house, built in 1728 and 1764, is the jewel of the town, and the drawing room, right, and library, below, are the two choicest rooms in this famous old family home.

*Stoller*

240

FROM OLD SALEM

ACROSS THE MOUNTAINS

TO KENTUCKY AND TENNESSEE

THEN DOWN THE MISSISSIPPI

FROM NATCHEZ TO NEW ORLEANS

AND OUT TO MONTEREY

# Dawn Service at Old Salem

Of all the places of this country's past, Old Salem in Winston-Salem, North Carolina, is one whose strains of European heritage are deeply intermingled with our own, in the cultural overtones of its worship, its architecture, and its music. Attractive at all times, it is especially so in the spring, a season ushered in at Easter by a custom that is typical of the town. Long before daylight groups of horn players begin winding and playing through the streets. The bell-like tones blow beautifully closer and die away in the distance, while other groups in turn take up the traditional tunes. "Sleepers awake!" is the cue they give. And other awakened sleepers follow the lamplit streets that lead to the church, where the sunrise service starts. The bricks of the houses are molded and baked from the soil of the town, and in many cases the walls and doorways are enriched with early Moravian ironwork. All ceremonies center around the noble old church, just as they do every Easter dawn. Next to the church, the Moravians' God's Acre is a scene at all times of park-like tranquility. An avenue of ancient trees cuts across the greensward where the gravestones lie flat and serene upon the grass. Every morning the stones pick up the first pink, level streaks of dawn, as they do at Easter when the horns play from separated points in the brightening burial ground; first one, then another, then another. . . . And then, as the sun itself appears, the congregation sings.

In the tavernkeeper's parlor: the chair and stove are from Pennsylvania; the tables and pottery are from Old Salem.

The tavernkeeper's bed curtains close to keep out drafts. His wife had her crewel frame by the window.

The Moravian tavern kitchen contains a *pair* of fireplaces, probably unique. The left is for baking and washing; the right one for cooking with a weight-driven spit-jack.

# The Vogler House

The Vogler parlor is all Moravian: from Mrs.
Vogler's sewing table, to the characteristically Salem
ear-wing chair and Daniel Welfare's portrait of the
tavernkeeper's wife and son. The dining room appears beyond.

Two little Vogler daughters, Lisette and Louisa, shared this bedroom, fitted out and furnished with typical Moravian things, and curtained and carpeted in typical Moravian fashion.

# KENTUCKY AND TENNESSEE

As a result of the great migration across the Alleghenies, mostly through Virginia and North Carolina, as well as by boat down the Ohio River, early houses are scattered all over both Kentucky and Tennessee—thinly in some parts, thickly in others. The concentrations of good early houses are most apparent around Lexington, founded in 1779, in the Blue Grass country of Kentucky, and around Nashville, founded the same year in the King Cotton country of Tennessee. The two Kentucky houses here represent the very early settlement of the territory of the two states. Stony Lonesome, out of Versailles, close to Lexington, was built in 1784; Malvern Hill, closer to Lexington, in 1790. The two Tennessee houses, on the other hand, represent the opulence and grandeur of the three decades preceding the Civil War: the Hermitage of 1831, and Belle Meade of 1853. All four houses reflect, each in its own fascinating way, the circumstances of the times in which they were built. Of course, these houses record the early history of their communities in an extremely personal fashion.

Because of its builder's celebrity, the Hermitage was bound to become the most celebrated. In 1831, a courier from Nashville appeared at the White House with word for the Jacksons that the first Hermitage, a plain brick mansion of about 1820, had been gutted by fire, but that the blackened walls still stood up strong. Word went back to start rebuilding right away and, as will be seen, a really resplendent mansion was the result.

# Stony Lonesome

The Indian bars still on the doors are reminders of its lonesomeness for long after Joel Dupuy built this house of off-white Kentucky River marble. Besides its blue grass and its bourbon, Kentucky is also famous for its early furniture, with which this whole house is furnished, including of course the bedroom, below.

The portico, a sign of the times, was put on the old white-painted brick house in 1820. The house stands in the midst of Kentucky's most beautiful pastoral country, further beautified with thoroughbreds grazing on that celebrated grass. The tides of migration which swept into this lovely land brought homebuilders from the seaboard states with seaboard ideas, accounting for Malvern's many colonial characteristics.

## Malvern Hill

The delicacy of the moldings in this fireplace corner of the family living room, left, and in the drawing room, right, is a sign of the eastern carpentry that created it.

250

# The Hermitage

The taste and personality of the Andrew Jacksons are all over the big double parlors and the bedroom, where everything now here belonged to them, although Rachel didn't live to see them settled in the rebuilt home. Mrs. Jackson's guitar and sewing box, filled with faded spools of silk, are in the far parlor. On the near mantel are silver luster vases sent to them by the Czar. The bed, with "A.J." on the spread, is the one in which the President died.

Size, color, and exuberance are the qualities that give the Belle Meade interiors their overwhelmingly grandiose quality. In the vast salon, the elaborate Belter chairs are prized features. The hallway for greetings and goodbys is on the grand scale. The double bedroom is divisible; the four-posters incomparable.

## Belle Meade in Nashville

The Belle Meade estate started with two log cabins built in 1798, by John Harding of Virginia. They still stand near the great mansion erected by his son, almost certainly from plans by William Strickland, who was in Tennessee designing the capitol. John Harding's son made the place one of the most prosperous in the state, enabling him, it is said, to give more than $5 million to the Confederate cause.

*Fowler*

# NATCHEZ TO NEW ORLEANS

Dunlieth is shown above, Stanton Hall opposite, something of the Elms, Gloucester and Lansdowne on the next two pages, and then Monteigne—just enough to get the feel of Natchez. Other names are just as romantic. Green Leaves, D'Evereux, Linden, Rosalie, Airlie, Mistletoe, and on and on—names and houses ornamenting the old town that stands high above the brown Mississippi, decorating the lush surrounding countryside. The Natchez Pilgrimage takes place in early spring. Down the river, the Louisiana plantations begin around St. Francisville, where Audubon stayed for a while to teach dancing and draw his birds. Greenwood was there.

Further along, on the river road behind the levee, are Houmas and San Francisco, and finally Ormond. Evergreen is across the river (by ferry) from Houmas and San Francisco. These are the four finest of the area. And after all this comes New Orleans, the one and only.

## Stanton Hall

It was typical of the flush times in Natchez in 1851, that the builder of Stanton Hall should have chartered a whole ship to bring materials and furnishings from Europe for his new home. The double drawing rooms open into a ballroom seventy-two feet long.

*Pratt*

As striking as most of the Natchez houses are outside, it is the rooms which elicit the "Ohs!" and "Ahs!" The back parlor of the Elms, for example, has its original Victorian furniture intact, still upholstered in the now seldom seen original Windsor patterns. Also seldom seen are the lily sconces on the mantel, and the rosewood escritoire.

The upholstered pieces in Gloucester's drawing room tell vividly how well Victorian took hold in Natchez.

The library at Gloucester has a mantel from France, Meissen from Germany, an English secretary, and paintings from Italy.

*owler*

The drawing room at Lansdowne represents the nineteenth century at its most fabulous, with a double set of French rosewood furniture, hand-painted wallpaper, carpet, cornices, and brocatels—all imported.

# Monteigne

Monteigne marks the close of the golden age of Natchez. Until the Civil War, the district was peopled with families who loved to live elegantly. The ships that carried their cotton to the eastern seaboard and to Europe carried them too, and brought them back with the finest of furnishings for their homes and with cosmopolitan ideas for this then remote community.

This bedroom at Monteigne is dominated by its *chinoiserie* chintz, its tester bed, and its rosewood chairs.

Monteigne's entrance hall, with its marble floor, harp-like balustrade, and hand-blocked scenic wallpaper.

*Fowler*

The great pillared plantation house looks
past the live oaks of the hexagonal *gar-
çonnière*, where the young male guests were
quartered.

The circular staircase at Houmas is seen
here, framed in a double doorway with
a semi-elliptical transom and linen-fold
carving.

# Houmas Plantation

The South Carolina Prestons inherited the lands here and built this splendid plantation in the 1840's. An arched patio connects the mansion with the caretaker's house that was here when the Prestons came. First a kitchen and servants quarters, it now has an office upstairs, and the dining room downstairs. At the right is one of the twin parlors now used as a bedroom.

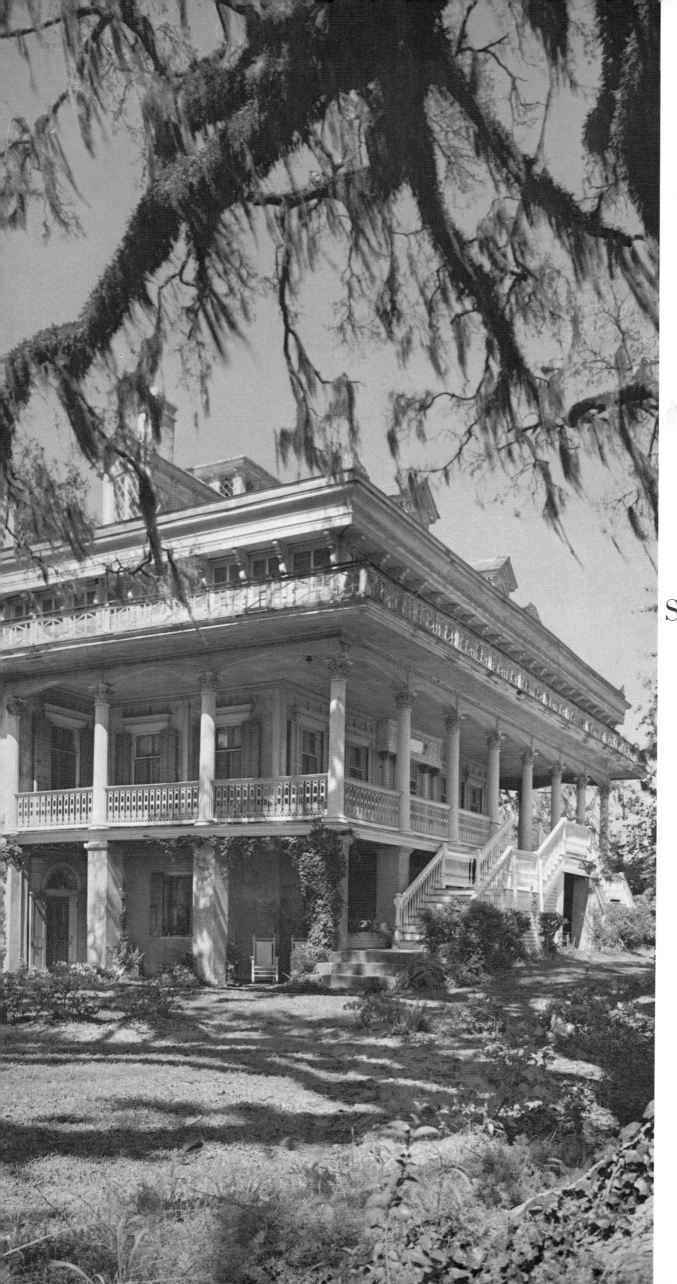

## San Francisco Plantation, L

In 1849, a man named Valein Marm
lion began the building of San Francis
but the physical and financial burde
were too much for his health, and he d
before he had quite finished it, leaving
a monument to his dream. Most splen
is the drawing room, one of four, whe
chief feature is Dominique Canov
painting on the cypress ceiling.

Stoller

# Evergreen Plantation

In the days of their glory, these plantations decorated both sides of the Mississippi, the whole length of Louisiana. Each was a private principality, with whole populations of help living in oak-lined avenues of cabins. Grouped around the pillared and galleried great house were kitchens, *garçonnières*, *pigeonniers*.

The bedroom of the owner who restored Evergreen, as well as the Gauche House, in New Orleans, a few pages farther along.

The original Evergreen kitchen is in a little building close by, as was common practice in large, early establishments in the South.

# Ormond Plantation

A few miles up the river from New Orleans, this plantation house looks very much as it always has, except for the later wings. Its colonnaded galleries are characteristic of the so-called "raised cottages" once so prevalent in the lower region of the great river.

# Greenwood Plantation

This great Greek Revival mansion, a hundred feet square, surrounded by twenty-eight columns of plastered brick, was built in the 1830's by the Barrow family from the Carolinas, complete with silver hardware and reflecting pond to mirror the house's glory. Now its glory is gone. A few weeks after the author took this picture, he received a telegram from the family: Greenwood had burned to the ground.

*Pratt*

# NEW ORLEANS

The streets in the Old Quarter have names like Iberville, Toulouse, Bienville, Bourbon, Dumaine and Chartres; and under the lacy galleries one hears snatches of Creole French. Dark passageways lead into patios filled with sunlight and palms. Both Thackeray and Mark Twain called this a Paris in America—which it isn't; but the flavor of the famous old Creole Quarter is decidedly French provincial. In the Garden District, the houses have an aura of ante-bellum elegance in settings of almost tropical lushness. Altogether, it makes a unique and romantic potpourri of French, Spanish, English, named New Orleans—with the accent on the *Or*. Pirate's Alley is on the right, more of the Old Quarter on the left.

*Pratt*

# The Gauche House

In the days when the Vieux Carré was almost exclusively Creole, and the Old Quarter was the special domain of the haughty French-Spanish set, John Gauche built this house at Esplanade and Royal, and hung its simple, four-square outside walls with cornices and galleries lined with lacy ironwork. The tallness of the windows gives away the wonderful ceiling heights within, upstairs and down.

The drawing room, left, is one of two on the first floor. The bedroom of the owner, right, recalls the splendor of earlier Creole days in New Orleans.

*Flannery*

# Garden District

This is one of the houses of James Gallier the younger, in the Garden District, where the elite of New Orleans built with elegance and grandeur before the Civil War; Doric verandahs below, Corinthian above. All the houses appear to be pillowed amid live oaks and palms even more regal than the houses themselves.

The banquet table stretches a full forty feet. The Washington portrait is by Gilbert Stuart's daughter Jane.

Here the Washington portrait is by Rembrandt Peale. The drawing-room ceiling is
sixteen feet high.

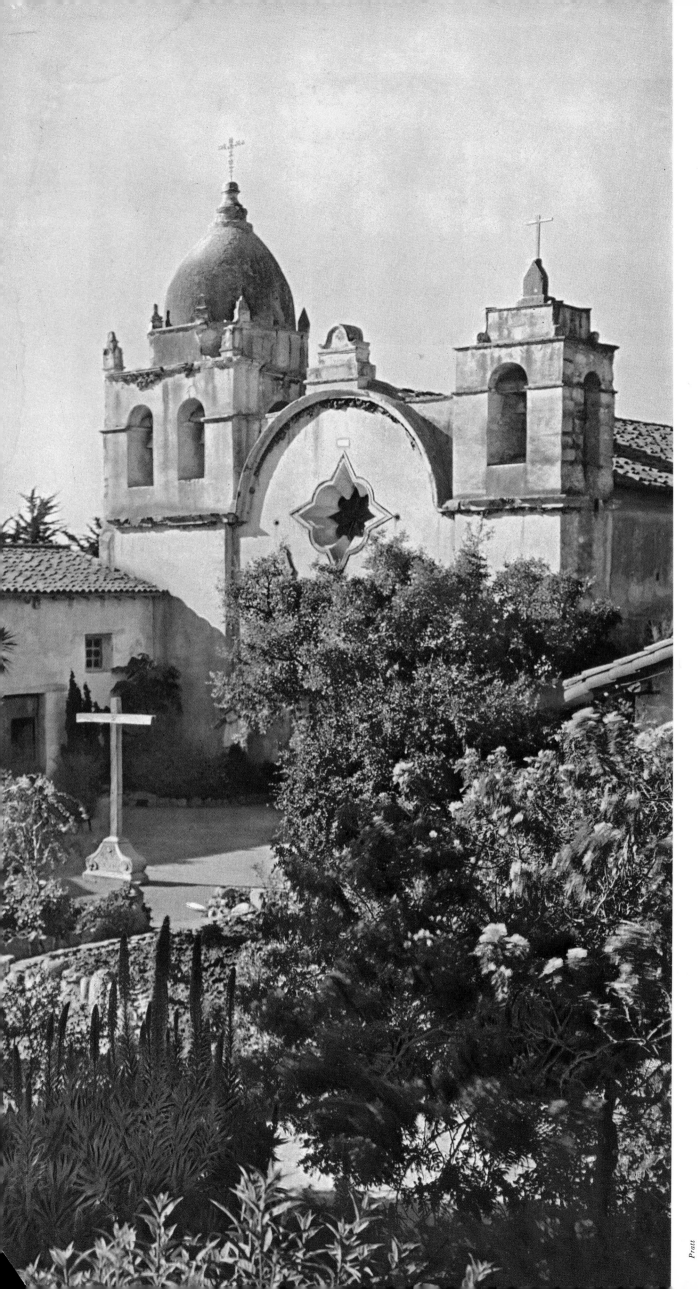

This beautiful adobe church was built in the 1790's at nearby Carmel. The work was done under the direction of Manuel Estevan Ruiz, a master mason from Spain. The heavy tile roof held until 1852, when, along with the fortunes of Monterey, it collapsed. Many of the tiles were taken to patch the roofs of that temporarily forsaken town. Now restored, its patio splendidly gardened, it is the ancient showpiece of the peninsula.

# MONTEREY

A painted yellow strip with arrows winds down the center of certain Monterey streets, leading eventually to every old house of any distinction in the city, such as the Casa Bonifacio, above, and the beautifully preserved old Customs House, below.

The early settlers merely molded blocks of mud from the ground, let them dry hard in the sun, and laid them up into walls—a trick that had worked its way up from Mexico, where adobe had been a building material for thousands of years.

277

*Pratt*

*Pratt*

## Casa Amesti

*Flannery*

This most delightful of adobes was built around 1830, by a rich rancher of the region, Don Jose Amesti, who then a little later gave it to his daughter Carmen when she married Don Santiago (born James) McKinley, a former Scottish sailor, who was left ashore off a whaler at San Francisco in the twenties and became a naturalized Mexican. The garden, and the restoration of the Casa, are a tribute to the taste of the late Frances Elkins, the well-known decorator, whose library is at the left, and her brother, the late David Adler, the famous architect, of Chicago. At Mrs. Elkins' behest, her Casa is now in the care of the National Trust for Historic Preservation.

278

# The Larkin House

When Thomas Oliver Larkin came from Boston in 1832, and built this house, he furthered a style which has become traditional with Monterey: long horizontal lines, hip roofs, and porches. The deep embrasured windows of the living room reveal the thickness of the adobe walls; the furniture the heritage of New England.

# INDEX